D1301878

DUE DATE

DEC 1 8 APR 0 8 1994			
OCT 3 1 2000			
			Printed in USA

SATAN

HIS MOTIVES AND METHODS

LEWIS SPERRY CHAFER

KREGEL PUBLICATIONS
Grand Rapids, Michigan 49501

Satan: His Motives and Methods, by Lewis Sperry Chafer. Published in 1990 by Kregel Publications, a division of Kregel, Inc., P. O. Box 2607, Grand Rapids, MI 49501, by special permission from Dallas Theological Seminary. All rights reserved.

Library of Congress Cataloging-in-Publication Data

Chafer, Lewis Sperry, 1871-1952.
 Satan: His motives and methods / Lewis Sperry Chafer.
  p.   cm.
 Reprint. Originally published: Rev. ed. 1919.

 1. Devil. 2. Spiritual Life—Presbyterian authors.
I. Title.
BT980.C5   1991   235'.47   90-20616
                                          CIP
ISBN   0-8254-2344-9 (pbk.)

        1 2 3 4 5 Printing/Year 94 93 92 91 90

        Printed in the United States of America

Contents

Foreword

If any word of mine shall add to the number of the readers of this book I shall be glad to have written it; and I sincerely wish that all believers, and especially all ministers and Christian workers, might in some way be led to read it.

The subject is vital to any right understanding of the age in which we live, and of the personal conflict which we wage, for the existence, personality, and power of Satan are awful facts and of immense present significance.

We walk in the midst of his snares, hear on every hand his doctrines proclaimed by men of blameless lives "transformed as the ministers of righteousness," and are allured by the pleasure, place and power of his perfectly organized world-system.

I know of no other book on Satan in which the dispensational aspects of the subject are so clearly stated, nor any other so severely biblical.

C. I. SCOFIELD

Introduction to the First Edition

The world has been willing to comply with the wishes and projects of Satan to the extent of ceasing to believe that he really exists, this unbelief being most advantageous in his present undertakings. Yet the opinions of men have never changed the facts of revelation, and, according to the Bible, Satan exists, still possessed with great power and influence over the affairs of men—a power and influence to be increasingly dreaded as this present age advances.

The teachings of the Scriptures on this important subject are but little understood by Christians and seem to be entirely outside the thought of the world. It is, therefore, to be expected that any attempt to present this truth will seem, to many, mere folly and fiction.

The name Satan has by no means been lost. It has, however, been associated with a most unscriptural fancy. Without reference to revelation, the world has imagined a grotesque being, fitted with strange trappings, who has been made the central character in works of fiction and theatrical performances, and by this relation to that which is unreal, the character of Satan has come to be considered only one of the myths of a bygone age.

The Bible reveals a detailed description of the person and career of Satan beginning with his creation, and includes his original condition, his fall, the development and manifestation

11

of his kingdom, and his final defeat and banishment. It presents a personage so mighty and so prominent in the world today that the Christian heart would fail, were it not for faith in the One who has triumphed over all principalities and powers.

This attempt to outline the Scripture teaching on this character will be undertaken under certain general conditions:

First—The authority of the Scriptures of both the Old Testament and the New will be accepted without question.

Second—Evidence will be drawn from the Word of God alone, since no final light can be found on this subject other than it has pleased God to reveal in the Bible.

Third—There will be no discussion as to the personality and existence of Satan, this being both assumed and taught in the Bible from Genesis to Revelation.

These pages are prepared especially for believers; knowing that this body of truth will be wholly unnoticed or rejected by the unsaved.

There has also been a deep sense of the seriousness of the undertaking: both because Satan, by his present direct power, would, if possible, hinder any larger understanding of his projects and purposes; and because so great a warning has fallen from the lips of Christ against the sin of ascribing to Satan the things which are really of God (Matt. 12:22–32). The work has, therefore, been undertaken with reliance upon the keeping and guiding power of the Spirit of God, and is presented with the prayer that believers may have a clearer understanding of this important body of truth and be able to say with Paul, "We are not ignorant of his devices." It is also desired that some clearer vision of this mighty foe may be had which will cause the child of God to realize the overwhelming power of his adversary and be constrained to "be strong in the Lord and in the power of his might" that greater victory may be had in the realization of the whole will of God.

1909

Introduction to the Revised Edition

In sending forth a new and revised edition of this book, there is abundant reason for gratitude to God for His blessing which has so manifestly rested upon the first edition during the ten years of its circulation. The book was published both in England and in the United States and the distribution has totalled over twenty-five thousand copies in ten years.

The message of this book is still timely. Every evidence of the close of the age, mentioned in the first edition, has been so increased during the past ten years that the statements there made and which seemed to some at the time of publishing to be extreme are now found to be inadequate to describe the present conditions in the world.

May the Lord our God continue to use this book to His Own glory and to the edification of His people is the prayer of the author.

1919

1

The Career of Satan

This chapter is a brief outline of the past, present and future of Satan, which is taken up at this point both that the following chapters may be more easily studied and because of the fact that those passages which deal most directly with his earliest condition are closely interwoven with predictions of his future and final defeat.

Revelation in regard to Satan begins with that dateless period between the perfect creation of the heavens and the earth (Gen. 1:1) and the desolating judgment which ended that period, when the earth became waste and empty (Gen. 1:2; Isa. 24:1; Jer. 4:23-26). One passage, Ezekiel 28:11-19, deals at length with Satan and his relation to that age. In this scripture, Satan is evidently described under the title of "The King of Tyrus." Like the Messianic Psalms—wherein the Psalmist is apparently referring to himself, though statements are made and conditions described that could only be connected with the Messiah, the Son of God—so, here, that which is addressed to "The King of Tyrus" is, by its character, seen to be a direct reference to the person of Satan; for no similar person to whom this description could apply is revealed in the Scriptures. In the previous as well as the following chapters the final judgment of Jehovah is pronounced upon the enemies of His chosen people. Satan is numbered among these enemies in 1 Chronicles 21:1; hence he naturally appears in this list.

Every sentence of this extended passage is a distinct revelation and is worthy of long and careful study. Only a passing reference can be made to it here. The passage is as follows:

"Moreover the word of the Lord came unto me, saying, Son of man, take up a lamentation upon the King of Tyrus, and say unto him, Thus saith the Lord God; Thou sealest up the sum, full of wisdom, and perfect in beauty. Thou hast been in Eden the garden of God; every precious stone was thy covering, the sardius, topaz, and the diamond, the beryl, the onyx, and the jasper, the sapphire, the emerald, and the carbuncle and gold: the workmanship of thy tabrets and of thy pipes was prepared in thee in the day that thou wast created. Thou art the anointed cherub that covereth; and I have set thee so: thou wast upon the holy mountain of God; thou hast walked up and down in the midst of the stones of fire. Thou wast perfect in thy ways from the day thou wast created, till iniquity was found in thee. By the multitude of thy merchandise they have filled the midst of thee with violence, and thou hast sinned: therefore I will cast thee as profane out of the mountain of God: and I will destroy thee, O covering cherub, from the midst of the stones of fire. Thine heart was lifted up because of thy beauty, thou hast corrupted thy wisdom by reason of thy brightness: I will cast thee to the ground, I will lay thee before Kings, that they may behold thee. Thou hast defiled thy sanctuaries by the multitude of thy iniquities, by the iniquity of thy traffic; therefore will I bring forth a fire from the midst of thee, it shall devour thee, and I will bring thee to ashes upon the earth in the sight of all them that behold thee. All they that know thee among the people shall be astonished at thee: thou shalt be a terror, and never shalt thou be any more."

This passage describes much of the early and latter career of Satan. Twice is his creation referred to. In verse fifteen it is stated that he was created perfect, and in verse thirteen that perfection is set forth in detail by the suggestive symbols of precious gems. He among all created beings was also "full of wisdom," "perfect in beauty," filling up the sum of perfection. In verse fourteen he is called "the anointed cherub that covereth." By this the purpose of the Creator is revealed. While Satan doubtless exercised some authority in the earth over the primal creation, the evident meaning of this verse is that Satan was created as a guard or protector to the throne of the most High. This is reasonable. Like the golden cherubim, covering

the visible mercy seat in the Holy of Holies of the earthly tabernacle, he was created a guard and covering cherub to the heavenly center of Glory. It is expressly stated that he was located
by the Most High upon the holy mountain of God, the mountain
of God being a symbol of the center of God's power, government, and eternal throne (Ps. 48:1; 68:15; Isa. 2:2). Over this
exalted throne Satan was set as a covering cherub. He is also
said to have been in "Eden, the garden of God," which is evidently another Eden than that in which Satan appeared as a
serpent. The Eden of Genesis was one of verdure and cosmic
beauty, while this is an Eden of "stones of fire." No king of
Tyrus was ever in either of the Edens mentioned in the Bible.
The title belongs most evidently to Satan. The whole passage
suggests a position of great authority for which he was created
and anointed; a position from which he fell, drawing with him
a host of beings over whom he had governing influence and
power.

Again, it is stated that Satan was perfect in all his ways from
the day he was created. It is important to notice both that he
was created, and that he was created perfect. Since he was
created, he is not self-existent, and never can be free from his
dependence upon the Creator. He may vainly propose to become independent, and even be permitted for a time to act
under that delusion; but that only delays the inevitable judgment
that awaits him. He was created perfect, or was a perfect fulfillment of the Creator's intention. Satan was a free moral agent,
capable of choosing evil but not obliged to do so. That he chose
evil must ever be his own condemnation, for the Creator had
surrounded him with sufficient motives for choosing the good.
Christ said of him, "He was a murderer from the beginning,
and abode not in the truth." It is thus revealed that Satan began
in the truth, but afterwards turned to a state wherein Christ
could go on to say of him, "There is no truth in him. When he
speaketh a lie, he speaketh of his own: for he is liar, and the
father of it" (John 8:44).

The crime of Satan is partly revealed in verse sixteen and
this is followed by an exact description of his final judgment as
it is predicted in the book of Revelation.

An important teaching of this passage is of Satan's first position and power—a power and wisdom sufficient to guard the throne of God from every possible enemy, and a glory and beauty that would become the highest officer in the Court of Heaven. By this revelation his present position and power may be estimated.

Another revelation next in importance is that of his crime which is clearly set forth in Isaiah 14:12-20. Before reading this passage it should be noticed that the prophet's vision of Satan, here recorded, is from the time of his final judgment, and the prophet is looking backward over Satan's whole career. Much that is still future is, therefore, referred to as though it were past. The passage is as follows:

"How art thou fallen from heaven, O Lucifer, son of the morning! How art thou cut down to the ground, which didst weaken the nations! For thou hast said in thine heart, I will ascend into heaven, I will exalt my throne above the stars of God: I will sit also upon the mount of the congregation, in the sides of the north: I will ascend above the heights of the clouds; I will be like the Most High. Yet thou shalt be brought down to hell, to the sides of the pit. They that see thee shall narrowly look upon thee, and consider thee, saying, Is this the man that made the earth to tremble, that did shake kingdoms; that made the world as a wilderness, and destroyed the cities thereof; that opened not the house of his prisoners? All the kings of the nations, even all of them, lie in glory, every one in his own house. But thou art cast out of thy grave like an abominable branch, and as the raiment of those that are slain, thrust through with a sword, that go down to the stones of the pit; as a carcass trodden under feet."

This heavenly title, "Lucifer, Son of the Morning," speaks of his first place in the celestial sphere, when the morning stars sang together and all the sons of God shouted for joy (Job 38:7). Christ is "The Bright and Morning Star," "The Sun of Righteousness" who shall yet arise with healing in His wings.

Has Satan ever fallen from heaven? The Word of God alone can answer this question. There are seven passages which should be considered in this connection:

1. *Ezekiel 28:16.* "Thou hast sinned: therefore I will cast thee as profane out of the mountain of God."

This prediction of judgment, with others which follow in the context and with which this casting out is associated, are predictions of the yet future judgments which are to fall upon Satan when he is banished to the pit and to the lake of fire. This passage does not teach that Satan was cast out of heaven at the time of his sin and as an immediate judgment for his sin.

2. *Isaiah 14:12.* "How art thou fallen from heaven, O Lucifer, son of the morning!"

This scripture, as has been stated, is also a description of that final judgment which is to be at the very end of Satan's career.

3. *Job 1:6.* "Now there was a day when the sons of God came to present themselves before the Lord, and Satan came also among them."

There seems to be nothing unusual in the appearance and presence of Satan among these heavenly beings. The passage discloses his position in heaven and also reveals the fact that, in the days of Job, Satan was free to go and come in the earth.

4. *Luke 22:31, 32.* "And the Lord said, Simon, Simon, behold, Satan hath desired to have you [obtained thee by asking], that he may sift you as wheat."

From this scripture we may conclude that Satan still had unchallenged access to the presence of God, in the day when this was spoken.

5. *Ephesians 6:11, 12, R.V.* "Put on the whole armour of God, that ye may be able to stand against the wiles [strategies] of the devil. For our wrestling is not against flesh and blood, but against the principalities, against the powers, against the world rulers of this darkness, against the spiritual hosts of wickedness in the heavenlies."

According to the Scriptures, throughout this age the believer must be prepared to war against a "spiritual host of wickedness in the heavenlies." The contributing evidence of this passage is to the effect that Satan is not yet cast out of heaven.

There is another revelation concerning Satan's present position in which it is declared that he now has access to the earth. "Be sober, be watchful: your adversary the devil, as a roaring lion, walketh about, seeking whom he may devour: whom withstand steadfast in the faith" (1 Pet. 5:8, 9). To this may also be added the revelation disclosed in the letter to the church at Pergamos, Revelation 2:13: "I know thy works, and where thou dwellest, even where Satan's seat [throne] is."

From these passages it may be concluded that the position of Satan in heaven and his freedom to go to and fro in the earth has not changed since the days of Job.

6. *Revelation 12:7-9*. "And there was war in heaven: Michael and his angels fought against the dragon; and the dragon fought and his angels, and prevailed not; neither was there place found any more in heaven. And the great dragon was cast out, that old serpent, called the Devil, and Satan, which deceiveth the whole world: he was cast out into the earth, and his angels were cast out with him."

This is the first passage in the Word of God which declares Satan to be actually banished from heaven. The passage also teaches that Satan remains in heaven until the time herein described.

According to the context it is that yet future time immediately preceding the setting up in the earth of the Kingdom of God and the power of His Christ.

7. *Luke 10:18*. "And he said unto them, I beheld Satan as lightning fall from heaven."

In the light of the passage just considered, it must be concluded that this was a prophetic utterance on the part of Christ, rather than a statement of history. The seventy had just returned with joy saying, "Lord, even the devils are subject unto us through thy name."

There is no question concerning the sufficiency of the power of God over Satan. It is only a question as to when that power will be exercised. The experience by the seventy of power over devils was only a suggestion to the mind of Christ of the mighty power which would yet be displayed in banishing Satan and his hosts from the heavenly sphere.

It is important to distinguish Satan's yet future physical banishment out of heaven from his moral fall. He undoubtedly fell morally at the moment of his sin, but his position throughout the ages, or until the return of the King, is in heaven. From this high position he has access both to God and to the earth.

There is not the slightest biblical basis for the theory that Satan or any of his hosts are now occupying hell. Though it is revealed that Satan is now a heavenly being, there is no evidence that there is agreement or fellowship between God and Satan. God's final judgments against Satan are not yet executed.

In like manner, God has not yet caused sin to cease in the earth; but the day is coming when He will.

Returning to Isaiah 14:12-20, the passage under consideration, we read of two aspects of Satan's present activity: He is first seen to be seeking to establish authority for himself and then he is seen to be the promoter of confusion and terror in the earth. He said, "I will exalt my throne above the stars of God," and it is also said of him: "Is this the man that made the earth to tremble, that did shake kingdoms; that made the world as a wilderness, and destroyed the cities thereof; that opened not the house of his prisoners?"

The crime of Satan is concisely stated in the fourteenth verse as being a purpose in his heart to become like the Most High. His heart was lifted up because of his beauty; he who was created and placed as the "Covering Cherub," with the high honor of guarding the throne of God, has corrupted his wisdom by reason of his brightness; he has struck at the throne which he was set to protect. It was a purpose in his heart which would require the time of the ages wholly to destroy. There could be but one Most High, and the purpose of Satan to become like Him could, naturally, be nothing less than an attempt to dethrone the Almighty.

Satan was the first being to manifest a will opposed to the will of God. In the above passage from Isaiah, five "I wills" are recorded of him:

"I will ascend into heaven."

"I will exalt my throne above the stars of God."

"I will sit also upon the mount."

"I will ascend above the heights of the clouds."

"I will be like the Most High."

The secret purpose in his heart reveals his method to be not a violent attack upon the throne; but, like Absalom, to steal the hearts of the unfaithful in the Kingdom of God, and, through subtlety, to gain a kingdom for himself. He would thus become an object of worship and attract attention from other beings to himself. To accomplish this, a hindering attitude must be assumed toward the purpose and projects of the Most High. No adequate appreciation can be formed of Satan's present projects and devices, and the motive that prompts them, without a clear understanding of his age-abiding attitude toward the Person of God.

There are two prominent events revealed in the history of Satan, falling within the period of time when he proposed in his heart to become like the Most High and his yet future banishment and execution. The first of these was his meeting with and triumph over the first Adam, when he wrested the scepter of authority from man, by securing man's loyal obedience to his own suggestion and counsel. This earthly scepter Satan held by the full right of conquest, seemingly without challenge from Jehovah, until the first advent of the Last Adam; this meeting of the Last Adam, Christ, with Satan being the second great event which is revealed during this period in his career. Only the unfolding of the coming ages can reveal the magnitude of this terrible conflict. A glimpse is revealed from time to time of the unceasing effort of Satan to triumph over the Last Adam, as he had triumphed over the first. He met the Lord Jesus in the wilderness, offering Him all he had gained from the first Adam, even the kingdoms of this world; if only he might become like the Most High, and receive the obedient worship and adoration of the Last Adam, the Son of God. Again he is seen voicing his attempt to dissuade the Christ from His sacrificial death, through the impetuous Peter (Matt. 16:23).

Since Satan had been in authority over the primal earth, it is reasonable to believe that he was filled with jealousy and hatred toward Adam, the newly created being to whom the earth authority was given. Satan made an attack upon Adam and wrested the scepter from his hand. God then decreed that there should be enmity between the seed of the woman and Satan. In tracing the line of the seed from Eden to Calvary, we may discern the constant attack of Satan upon this line of seed, and note as well the unfailing divine protection and intervention. The first born of Adam is mentioned in 1 John 3:12 as, "Cain, who was of that wicked one and slew his brother." But God raised up Seth. Thus it ever was.

However victorious Satan may have been over the first Adam, it is certain that he met a complete and final judgment and sentence in the Last Adam, and that the bruising of the serpent's head, which was a part of the Adamic covenant, was realized. Referring to His cross, Jesus said, "Now is the judgment of this world, now shall the prince of this world be cast out" (John 12:31). And again in John 16:11, "Of judgment because the prince of this world is judged." Still another scriptural testimony to this great defeat of Satan is recorded in Colossians 2:13-15: "Having forgiven you all trespasses; blotting out the handwriting of ordinances that was against us, which was contrary to us, and took it out of the way, nailing it to the cross; and having spoiled principalities and powers, he made a show of them openly, triumphing over them in it." It is, therefore, clear that, though Satan may have triumphed over the first Adam and thereby become the god and prince of this world, he himself was perfectly and finally triumphed over and judged by the Last Adam in the cross.

It is quite possible, however, that a sentence may be pronounced and made known some time before the sentence is actually executed. During such an interval a criminal is said to be under sentence awaiting his execution which some higher authority has decreed. This period of sentence is that in which Satan appears the present age, which age had its beginning with the cross. Execution of this sentence would have banished him forever. That he is not banished is revealed in the fact that he, even after his judgment in the cross, is referred to in the Scriptures as still being in authority over this world.

An illustration of Satan's present relation to this world may be taken from the history of Saul and David. It is natural that David, the first to occupy the Davidic throne, should be a type of Christ, predicted to be the last and most glorious occupant of that throne (Luke 1:31-33). As there was a period between the anointing of David and the final banishment of Saul, in which Saul reigned as a usurper, though under divine sentence and David was the God-appointed king: in like manner there is now a similar period in which Satan rules as a usurper, though under sentence; and the actual occupation of Christ's throne is still future. In this period Satan, the rejected monarch, still rules;

hunting to the death all those who have allied themselves with Christ, the God-anointed King.

Why Satan is thus allowed to continue his reign is perhaps but partly revealed. The real Church which is the Bride of Christ, is to sit with Him upon His throne (Rev. 3:21; 1 Cor. 6:2, 3; Matt. 19:28), and the present age must continue until that glorious heavenly people are gathered out from the world. Again, it seems the course of God's purpose to make a sufficient and final trial of every claim of His adversaries; and when this age, with all its developments, shall have passed by, every mouth will be stopped, and the whole world and Satan will know their own failure and sin before God. They will stand self-condemned, and nothing could accomplish this but the testing, by actual trial, of all the self-sufficient claims of Satan and man. The sin of man has brought him under sentence too, and grace alone withholds his immediate execution (John 3:18; Rom. 5:18, 19). Though the day of execution is, in the purpose of God delayed, it is, nevertheless, sure; and the time is fast approaching when an awful destruction of self-enthroned beings will be executed, and He alone shall reign, whose right it is to reign, "for he must reign until he hath put all enemies under his feet" (1 Cor. 15:25). The Kingly Son shall yet arise and claim the nations of the earth and "break them with a rod of iron, and dash them in pieces as a potter's vessel" (Ps. 2:9).

Another probable reason for the delay in the termination of evil in the world and the execution of judgment upon Satan is that the presence of evil in the world provides the Christian with a ceaseless conflict by which he can alone gain the character of an overcomer. This character is vital and is priceless in the sight of God.

So, also, the Christian is privileged to be a witness. (The word witness is from the same root as martyr.) By his faithful testimony against the enemy of God, the believer is able to gain his crown and reward. This, too, is priceless in the sight of God.

It would seem that, until near the end of his career, Satan cherishes the expectation of actually accomplishing his purpose (though the demon testimony of Matthew 8:29 is suggestive on this point). Preceding his banishment to the pit, he is violently cast out of heaven and into the earth, according to Revelation

12:7-12; and his activity from that time on is limited to that sphere. He is no longer granted access to God. The passage is as follows:

"And there was war in heaven: Michael and his angels fought against the dragon; and the dragon fought and his angels, and prevailed not; neither was there place found any more in heaven. And the great dragon was cast out, that old serpent, called the Devil, and Satan, which deceiveth the whole world: he was cast out into the earth, and his angels were cast out with him. And I heard a loud voice saying in heaven, Now is come salvation and strength, and the kingdom of our God, and the power of His Christ: for the accuser of our brethren is cast down, which accuseth them before God day and night. And they overcame him by the blood of the Lamb, and by the word of their testimony; and they loved not their lives unto the death. Therefore rejoice, ye heavens, and ye that dwell in them. Woe to the inhabitants of the earth and of the sea! For the devil is come down unto you, having great wrath, because he knoweth that he hath but a short time."

Here Satan is pictured as being in great wrath as he is banished from heaven into the earth, "knowing that he has but a short time." After this short time, in which occurs the great tribulation in the earth, Satan is bound and cast into a pit, this being an event in the glorious return of Christ to the earth, where He will reign on the throne of His father David for a thousand years. Satan is confined to the pit during the same period, at the end of which he is released for "a little season." He then gathers an army for a last attack upon the government and people of God, which ends in his being banished to the lake of fire, where he will meet his final and long predicted doom. These events are clearly stated in their order in the nineteenth and twentieth chapters of Revelation. A portion of this scripture is here given:

"And I saw an angel come down from heaven, having the key of the bottomless pit [abyss] and a great chain in his hand. And he laid hold on the dragon, that old serpent, which is the Devil, and Satan, and bound him a thousand years. And cast him into the bottomless pit [abyss], and shut him up, and set a seal upon him, that he should deceive the nations no more, till the thousand years should be fulfilled: and after that he must be loosed a little season. And when the thousand years are expired, Satan shall be loosed out of his prison, and shall go out to deceive the nations which are in the four quarters of the earth, Gog and Magog, to gather them together to battle: the number of whom is as the sand of the sea. And they went up on the breadth of the earth, and compassed the camp of the saints about, and the beloved city: and fire came down from God out of heaven, and devoured them. And the devil that deceived them was cast into the lake of fire and brimstone, where the beast and the false prophet are, and shall be tormented day and night for ever and ever" (Rev. 20:1-10).

Satan is thus revealed as having been created perfect in all his ways, mighty in power, and full of beauty and wisdom. While thus privileged, he proposed in his heart a stupendous project—himself to become like the Most High. Though remaining in heaven and having access to God, he is seen wresting the world scepter from man; ruling as the god of this world, until the judgment of the cross; and after that he still rules as a usurper. At the end of the age he is cast out of heaven into the earth, with further access to the former denied; from thence to the pit; and finally is banished to the lake of fire forever.

This review of the career of Satan is made at this point in order to call attention to the direct and mighty influence he exerts upon the affairs of this world according to his varying positions and freedom.

After Satan rebelled, humanity, too, was thrown into an abnormal and almost universal attitude of independence toward God; and this continues beyond the cross to the end of the age with increasing confusion and darkness. The only exception to this rebellion is the little company of believers, and how real is the tendency to the self-governed life of the old nature, even among these! When Satan is cast out of heaven and limited to the earth, there is the tribulation upon the earth of which Jesus speaks in Matthew 24:21, and which is also referred to in Daniel 12:1. When Satan is bound and put in the pit, and the promised Kingdom of Christ has come, there is peace covering the earth as waters cover the face of the deep.

Can it be doubted that this mighty being is a living power, acting directly over the affairs of men, even in this self-glorying age?

2

The Ages

It is a conspicuous fact that the comparatively few errors and inconsistencies in translation found in the English Authorized Version of the New Testament serve to hinder, directly or indirectly, any clear understanding of the teachings of the Scriptures in regard to the conditions and relationships of the world at the present time. Even the Revised Version did not greatly relieve this confusion beyond the addition of some helpful marginal renderings. It would seem, if it were possible, that Satan, the author of confusion and the only one advantaged by it, had been able in some subtle way to keep in darkness that which otherwise would be light, thus preventing a revelation of his own projects.

The continuation of these misleading translations is most evident in the unqualified use of the English word "world." This word which, in common usage, has a limited meaning is used by the translators as the one English rendering for at least three widely differing ideas in the Greek text. Hence if the truth contained in this important body of scripture is to be understood, the student must not only know the various meanings which are expressed by the one word, but also be able to determine the correct use of the word in any single instance. This necessary effort to understand the real meaning of many passages has, therefore, placed the simple truth they contain beyond the average reader of the Bible.

The English word "world" as used in the New Testament may mean a distinct period of time, commonly known as an age (as its original is a few times translated) or it may refer to the things created—the earth, its inhabitants, or their institutions. Two of these original meanings are used in connection with this present time.

First, as to an age, or period of time: The ages are often referred to in the Scriptures, and the study of the exact conditions and purposes of each of them is not a fanciful pursuit, but is rather the only adequate foundation for any true knowledge of the Bible. It is not possible to consider all the ages in this chapter, but only such as may be confused with the present one.

The age of law, which began with the giving of the law at Mount Sinai and ended, approximately, with the death of Christ, is mentioned by Zacharias in his prophecy at the birth of John: "As he spake by the mouth of his holy prophets which have been since the world [*age*] began" (Luke 1:70). The same period is referred to by Peter in Acts 3:21: "Whom the heavens must receive until the restitution of all things, which God hath spoken by the mouth of all his prophets since the world [*age*] began." These references, it will be seen, are not to the creation of the world, as the English rendering would indicate; but to the beginning of that particular period in which the prophets spake.

The present age of grace, in which the grace of God has had its appearing unto salvation, began where the age of law ended, or with the death of Christ; and will continue until He comes again. The duration of this age is suggested by the communion table which, being peculiar to this age, will continue to its end. Of this sacrament it is said: "As oft as ye eat this bread, and drink this cup, ye do show the Lord's death till he come" (1 Cor. 11:26).

As a distinct period of time this age is mentioned by the word "world" no less than forty times in the New Testament. A few of these passages follow: "And whosoever speaketh a word against the son of man, it shall be forgiven him: but whosoever speaketh against the Holy Spirit, it shall not be forgiven him, neither in this world [*age*], neither in the world [*age*] to come" (Matt. 12:32). "And as he sat upon the Mount of Olives, the disciples came to him privately, saying, Tell us, when shall these things be and what shall be the sign of thy coming, and of the end of the world [*age*]?" (Matt. 24:3). "The field is the world [*men*]; the good seed are the children of the kingdom; but the tares are the children of the wicked one; the enemy that sowed them is the devil; the harvest is the end of the world [*age*] and the reapers are the angels" (Matt. 13:38, 39). "And, lo, I am with you alway, even unto the end of the world [*age*] (Matt. 28:20). "For the children of this world [*age*] are in their generation wiser than the children of light" (Luke 16:8). "And set him at his own right hand in the heavenlies, far above all principality, and power, and might, and dominion, and every name that is named, not only in this world [*age*], but that which is to come" (Eph. 1:20, 21). "We should live soberly, righteously, and godly in this present world [*age*]" (Titus 2:12). By these and many other passages, it may be seen that the present age is a particular limited period of time in which special conditions are to prevail, and definite purposes are to be realized.

Judging from the mass of Christian writings and from utterances in public address and prayer, this age is assumed by many, without question, to be the kingdom of Christ, though no scripture is found to warrant that conclusion.

There is a kingdom of God which embraces the entire universe, over which God is enthroned, and to this kingdom every enemy must finally be brought back to original subjection and adjustment, or be banished forever. This final victory is described in 1 Corinthians 15:24, 25: "Then cometh the end, when he [Christ] shall have delivered up the kingdom to God, even the Father; when he shall have put down all rule and all authority and power. For he must reign, till he hath put all enemies under his feet."

There is a still more extensive body of scripture which anticipates a literal kingdom of righteousness and peace upon the earth; this theme being the burden of the Old Testament prophets, and was announced by John the Baptist, by Christ and His disciples. This announcement was simple and plain: "The kingdom of heaven is at hand." The expression "at hand" here used is significant, indicating not necessarily the immediate future, though the kingdom was definitely offered to that generation; but that the earthly kingdom was the next event which had been clearly announced by the prophets. When the Messiah had been positively rejected by the Jews, He began alone, without even the sympathy of His disciples, to unfold this forthcoming mystery-age which had been kept secret in the councils of God. The purpose of this age was more perfectly revealed to Paul, the first messenger to the Gentiles. Of this revelation of a hitherto unknown age and its purpose, Paul writes in Ephesians 3:1-11: "For this cause I, Paul, the prisoner of Jesus Christ for you Gentiles, if ye have heard of the dispensation of the grace of God which is given to me to you-ward: how that by revelation he made known unto me the mystery; (as I wrote afore in few words, whereby, when ye read, ye may understand my knowledge in the mystery of Christ) which in other ages was not made known unto the sons of men, as it is now revealed unto his holy apostles and prophets by the Spirit; that the Gentiles should be fellow-heirs, and of the same body, and partakers of his promise in Christ by the gospel: whereof I was made a minister, according to the gift of the grace of God given unto me by the effectual working of his power. Unto me, who am less than the least of all saints, is this grace given, that I should preach among the Gentiles the unsearchable riches of Christ; and to make all men see what is the fellowship of the mystery, which from the beginning of the world hath been hid in God, who created all things by Jesus Christ: to the intent that now unto the principalities and powers in heavenly places might be known by the church the manifold wisdom of God, according to the eternal purpose which he purposed in Christ Jesus our Lord."

The same truth is emphasized in Romans 16:25: "Now to him that is of power to stablish you according to my gospel, and the preaching of Jesus Christ, according to the revelation of the mystery, which was kept secret since the world began."

This new age of the Gentiles was also to have its hope centered in Jesus Christ, but in His sacrificial death rather than His kingly reign. It was to be an age in which the Gentiles were to be visited and a people called out from them for His own Person (Acts 15:14) and these people, who are the real Church, were to be built together upon a rock (Matt. 16:18). Their glorious salvation and final heavenly perfection were to rest only on His perfect and finished work for them. By this divine transformation, He would secure out of all nations, both Gentiles and Jews, a heavenly people; wholly fitted in quality to be His own body, His heavenly bride, and a kingdom of priests unto God.

All this, though not revealed in past ages, was known in the councils of God (Acts 15:18), and is parenthetical in the history of the Jew. It is a delay of their earthly kingdom and in no way its fulfillment or substitute.

Want of knowledge concerning the right divisions of truth is also evident in the general impression that God has cast off His people, the Jews, and that the Gentiles are their rightful successors and the recipients of the blessings of their unfulfilled prophecies. This confusion is due to a failure to distinguish between this and the following age.

Two distinct lines of seed were promised to Abraham. One, an earthly seed, to be like the dust of the earth, without number (Gen. 13:16), centered wholly in the earth by a relationship of physical generation: the other seed were likened to the stars of heaven, without number (Gen. 15:5), centered wholly in the heavenlies by a relationship of Spirit regeneration, which is the present answer of God to all true Abrahamic faith (Rom. 4:1-5). The earthly people found their origin in the physical fatherhood of Abraham: while the heavenly people find theirs in the shed blood of Christ. One had an earthly history from Abraham's time to their dispersion among the Gentiles—a history which will yet be resumed and the everlasting covenants fulfilled in the faithfulness of God: the other has a transient earthly pilgrimage from the cross continuing until their completion as a separated people; when they will be caught up to meet and marry their Bridegroom, and be forever with the Lord (1 Thess. 4:13-17).

To one, Christ is the coming glorious Messiah, who will sit upon the throne of His father, David (Luke 1:31-33), in a literal earthly kingdom (else all scripture language fails): to the other, He is the glorious Head of the Body, and coming Bridegroom. One of these lines of seed will be the favored subjects in the earthly kingdom: while the other will be in His bosom as a bride, and be associated with Him in His reign (1 Cor. 6:2; Rev. 3:21).

As these two lines of seed are everywhere distinct, there

must be at least two separate ages for the accomplishment of these ends. What, then, are these ages?

If it is believed that an earthly kingdom, with Messiah as King, is promised the Jew, it must also be admitted that the Jew is not now enjoying that kingdom; nor has he had any semblance of a kingdom during all the centuries since his dispersion among the Gentiles. This age cannot, therefore, be the predicted earthly kingdom of Christ. Turning to Acts 15:13-18, a description of the present age and that which will follow is found. The passage is as follows: "And after they had held their peace, James answered, saying, Men and brethren, hearken unto me: Simeon hath declared how God at the first did visit the Gentiles, to take out of them a people for his name. And to this agree the words of the prophets; as it is written, after this I will return, and will build again the tabernacle of David, which is fallen down; and I will build again the ruins thereof, and I will set it up; that the residue of men might seek after the Lord, and all the Gentiles, upon whom my name is called, saith the Lord, who doeth all these things. Known unto God are all his works from the beginning of the world."

It is recorded that after His resurrection Jesus was seen for forty days by the apostles whom He had chosen, and during this time He was speaking to them concerning the kingdom of God. It was natural, therefore, for them to inquire, at the end of those days, "Lord, wilt thou at this time restore again the kingdom unto Israel?" (Acts 1:6) and they had full warrant from the prophets to expect that great event when their Messiah came. They had not, however, grasped the meaning of the then dawning age of the gathering out of the Bride, and in this passage they are seen adjusting themselves to the newly revealed divine program, and recognizing the God-appointed delay in the predicted earthly kingdom.

In Acts 15 just referred to, the purpose of two distinct ages is set forth. The first age is described as the "visiting of the Gentiles," that from among them a heavenly people may be called out, and is a description of this present age, which had its beginning in the very generation in which this passage was written, for no previous age could meet these conditions. The second age, here described, is that of a rebuilding of the Davidic order which is clearly separated from the former age by the return of Christ. This same order of events is also carefully maintained wherever these events are referred to in the Bible, and any confusion of the order is a positive violence to the truth. The revealed consummation of this Gentile age is always the return of Christ, who comes first to receive His own; then to render judgment upon all the nations, and to bind the enemy and place him in the pit. The same return of Christ is the necessary preliminary event before any kingdom of righteousness and peace can be realized upon the earth. No amount of enlightened sentiment can establish the kingdom without the King; and no universal blessedness can be experienced in this world until the enemy is dethroned and banished. Sadly has the world failed to include these two necessary divine movements, in its vain dream and godless attempt at a perfected universe!

The purpose of this age is then defined as the visiting of the Gentiles to call out of them a people for His name; the called out people being the true Church (as that word signifies), which is made up of all the saved ones who have been saved since the Day of Pentecost at which time the Spirit came to unite them into one body and to indwell them. They are the heavenly people, regenerate and complete in Christ, their Bridegroom and living Head.

When this age is considered as the kingdom of Christ, it is usually thought of as in a state of development. This is a necessary conclusion in view of the presence of sin and failure in the world. But the setting up of the earthly kingdom is never described as the result of a process. The Bible deals conclusively with this question.

In Daniel 2:34-35, an image is described, which is defined as being a symbol of the then dawning Gentile world power (which power is still continuing, Luke 21:24). The image is here made to represent both the development of world rule and its final ending. The image by its various sections previews the successive world-powers that were to be. The end is then precipitated by a shattering blow from a stone, "cut out without hands." By the same inspired interpretation, the "stone" becomes both a symbol of superhuman power, being "cut out without hands," and a type of Christ, the Ancient of Days, in His coming to the earth as a resistless Monarch, banishing all rule and authority. A portion of the whole passage reads thus: "Thou sawest till that a stone was cut out without hands, which smote the image upon his feet that were of iron and clay, and brake them to pieces. Then was the iron, the clay, the brass, the silver, and the gold, broken to pieces together, and became like the chaff of the summer threshing-floor; and the wind carried them away, that no place was found for them: and the stone that smote the image became a great mountain, and filled the whole earth" (Dan. 2:34-35).

This being a divinely interpreted prophecy concerning the extent and ending of the present Gentile age, it should be noted that the stone (Christ) strikes the image (the world power) with one destructive blow, and at the time when it has become fully developed. The blow is struck on the part of the image which is last formed. The great image is thus instantly and violently broken to pieces and is even blown away "like the chaff of the summer threshing-floor." In like manner, according to this prophecy, the whole Gentile rule will suddenly be broken and will vanish.

It should also be noted from these symbols that the stone does not "become a mountain and fill the whole earth" until the great image has been scattered to dust. From this it is certain that there can be no development of the kingdom of Christ on the earth before the final breaking of the kingdoms of the earth. This same order is recognized throughout all prophecy. The King suddenly returns as lightning shining from one part of heaven to the other; Satan is violently seized and cast into prison; and a nation is born at once. The second Psalm connects the kingly reign of Christ—the time when He is set upon the holy hill of Zion—with the time when He shall claim the nations of the earth and "break them with a rod of iron and dash them in pieces as a potter's vessel." Also in Matthew 25:31, "when He sits on the throne of his glory" the "blessed of the Father" are called to enter the kingdom prepared for them from the foundation of the world. And in Revelation 12:7-12, where Satan is cast out into the earth and the execution of his sentence is begun, the announcement is made by a loud voice in heaven, "Now is come salvation, and strength, and the kingdom of our

God, and the power of his Christ." There is no evidence of a gradual process here; all is sudden and decisive.

Again, this age is not the coming earthly kingdom, for nowhere are the promised conditions of that kingdom now to be found. The Old Testament prophecies contain long and detailed descriptions of that glorious time. God's ancient people shall become the chosen nation, restored to their own land; the enemy shall be banished; the earth shall be purified, and blossom as a rose. "The wolf also shall dwell with the lamb, and the leopard shall lie down with the kid; and the calf and the young lion and the fatling together; and a little child shall lead them. And the cow and the bear shall feed; their young ones shall lie down together, and the lion shall eat straw like the ox. And the sucking child shall play on the hole of the asp, and the weaned child shall put his hand on the cockatrice den. They shall not hurt or destroy in all my holy mountain: for the earth shall be full of the knowledge of the Lord, as the waters cover the sea" (Isa. 11:6-9). "And in that day will I make a covenant for them with the beasts of the field, and with the fowls of heaven, and with the creeping things of the ground: and I will break the bow and the sword and the battle out of the earth, and will make them to lie down safely" (Hos. 2:18). "And it shall come to pass in that day, that the mountains shall drop down new wine, and the hills shall flow with milk, and all the rivers of Judah shall flow with waters, and a fountain shall come forth of the house of the Lord, and shall water the valley of Shittim" (Joel 3:18). "Sing and rejoice, O daughter of Zion: for, lo, I come, and I will dwell in the midst of thee, saith the Lord. And many nations shall be joined to the Lord in that day, and shall be my people: and I will dwell in the midst of thee, and thou shalt know that the Lord of hosts hath sent me unto thee" (Zech. 2:10, 11). "Thus saith the Lord of hosts; in those days it shall come to pass, that ten men shall take hold out of all languages of the nation, even shall take hold of the skirt of him that is a Jew, saying, We will go with you: for we have heard that God is with you" (Zech. 8:23). "For behold, I create new heavens and a new earth: and the former shall not be remembered, nor come into mind. But be ye glad and rejoice forever in that which I create: for behold, I create Jerusalem a rejoicing, and her people a joy. And I will rejoice in Jerusalem, and joy in my people: and the voice of weeping shall be no more heard in her, nor the voice of crying. There shall be no more thence an infant of days, nor an old man that hath not filled his days: for the child shall die an hundred years old; but the sinner being an hundred years old shall be accursed. And they shall build houses, and inhabit them; and they shall plant vineyards, and eat the fruit of them" (Isa. 65:17-21). "Then the eyes of the blind shall be opened, and the ears of the deaf shall be unstopped. Then shall the lame man leap as an hart, and the tongue of the dumb sing: for in the wilderness shall waters break out, and streams in the desert" (Isa. 35:5, 6). "But this shall be the covenant that I will make with the house of Israel. After those days, saith the Lord, I will put my law in their inward parts, and write it in their hearts; and will be their God and they shall be my people. And they shall teach no more every man his neighbor, and every man his brother, saying, Know the Lord: for they shall all know me, from the least of them unto the greatest of them, saith the Lord: for I will forgive their iniquity, and I will remember their sins no more" (Jer. 31:33, 34). "For unto us a child is born, unto us a son is given: and the government shall be upon his shoulder: and his name shall be called Wonderful, Counsellor, The mighty God, The everlasting Father, The Prince of Peace. Of the increase of his government and peace there shall be no end, upon the throne of David, and upon the kingdom, to order it, and to establish it with judgment and with justice from henceforth even forever. The zeal of the Lord of hosts will perform this" (Isa. 9:6, 7). "He shall be great, and shall be called the Son of the Highest: and the Lord God shall give unto him the throne of his father David; and he shall reign over the house of Jacob forever; and of his kingdom there shall be no end" (Luke 1:32, 33). "And he shall set up an ensign for the nations, and shall assemble the outcasts of Israel, and gather together the dispersed of Judah from the four corners of the earth" (Isa. 11:12). "And he shall judge among many people, and rebuke strong nations afar off; and they shall beat their swords into plowshares, and their spears into pruning hooks: nation shall not lift up a sword against nation, neither shall they learn war any more. But they shall sit every man under his vine and under his fig tree; and none shall make them afraid: for the mouth of the Lord of hosts hath spoken it" (Micah 4:3, 4).[1]

Though blessings abound in the individual heart, and though the predicted conditions which are to precede the return of the King are everywhere present, the Messianic kingdom is not yet set up in the earth. It is still "the times of the Gentiles."

---

1. A more extended discussion of the plan and purpose of God in the ages will be found in the author's book, *The Kingdom in History and Prophecy*.

3

The Course of This Age

It is necessary to distinguish between rightly dividing the Word of Truth, and a critical attitude toward that word; the former being an important duty in the believer's life, according to 2 Timothy 2:15, while the latter may easily become a wicked and misleading display of unbelief and the wisdom of this world (1 Cor. 1:19).

Personal interest in the Word of God usually begins with the first understanding of its real divisions; and no one is prepared to understand the providence of God who does not first come to know something of the purpose of God as marked off by these divisions. Especially is this necessary, as has been stated, for any clear understanding of the present age.

Again, the power and force of the whole body of scripture must depend, in a large measure, upon a belief in unfulfilled prophecy. Such a belief is not general, even among Christians. They believe that Christ came in the flesh, suffered, died, and rose again, because that is all now a matter of history; but that belief is not greatly influenced by the fact that this was all exactly foretold by the prophets. Let those who are free to condemn the pious Jew for not recognizing the fulfillment of prophecy in the first advent of Christ, beware lest they fail rightly to interpret the signs of these times, or look with positive unbelief upon the stupendous events that, according to prophecy, are imminent today. It seems a sore test of faith to believe that which is predicted for the present age, though those predictions are being fulfilled in every particular. This prevailing attitude of unbelief usually arises from one of two errors: either Satan has been so estimated that it seems impossible for him to be the promoter of anything that is moral or good (of this error more will be said in the following chapters), or the exact meaning and purpose of this age has been disbelieved or misunderstood; and because of these conditions many enthusiastic Christians are found to be, not only working toward unscriptural and hopeless ends, but are actually contributing to the confusion and darkness that is prevalent today.

The purpose and course of this age are not matters of prediction alone. Almost two thousand years of history may be considered in the light of these predictions; and while the age is not yet complete, and much that is reserved for the last days may be still future, enough of prophecy has now been fulfilled to indicate the certain fulfillment of all.

Since there has been no universal conversion of men in even the most favored locality, it is evident that, thus far, there has been a separating and calling out of a few from the many; and the divine purpose, as revealed in the Scriptures, which is to gather out a people from the Gentiles for His own name, has been verified. The blessing of God has been upon world-wide evangelism, rather than upon any fruitless attempts at world-wide conversion; for the individual or church that has become self-centered has, to that degree, sacrificed the power and blessing of the presence of Christ which was promised in Matthew 28:20: "Go ye therefore, and disciple all nations"—"Lo, I am with you alway, even unto the end of the age."

Again, the formation of the kingdom has not been discernible in the present age. The Jews, to whom alone the promises of an earthly kingdom belong, have continued a separate people under the unseen hand of God, without a country, or a vestige of national life. Certainly none of the predicted and necessary events accompanying the establishment of their kingdom have been experienced, nor is there any trace of its promised blessings. The fact that the Jews are now about to receive the title and possession of their native land, argues nothing for this age, more than that its end is very near, and that the way for their coming Messiah and national glory is being prepared. Just so, the conspicuous fact that all the marvelous present development of the resources of the earth has been limited to about the last sixtieth of the present history of the age may be evidence that the earth's return to her former glory is already in preparation.

Belief in the revealed course of this age can be, therefore, verified by history as well as based on the predictions of scripture.

The present age differs from all others by reason of the admixture of opposing classes of people; there being two divisions (not including the Jew as a nation) living and acting together, who are, nevertheless, removed from each other by a gulf that is immeasurable. This fact necessitates many careful distinctions and special injunctions which are peculiar to the age.

The fact that these two widely differing classes are present together, and are to continue so to the end of the age, is the teaching of the seven parables in the thirteenth chapter of Matthew. Very much, therefore, depends upon the correct interpretation of these parables. Their meaning has been somewhat hidden by the use of the word "world" where reference is made to this period of time; and the fact that the conditions described are true of this age only, has not been generally realized.

These seven parables are but a description of the unfolding and development of these mixed elements to be found in Christendom throughout this age. A similar prophecy, adding fuller historical details, is again proclaimed by Christ from the Glory, in the messages to the seven churches of Asia (Rev. 2 and 3). In these seven letters to organized existing churches, besides other applications, is revealed an outline of the history of Christendom for this entire age. The first two parables of Matthew 13 are interpreted by Christ Himself, and His interpretation of these sheds light on all that follows.

Christ is the Sower in both the first and second of these parables, and the sowing is continued by His servants throughout this age. The field is the world of men, which reveals a marked change from the responsibility of the Jewish age which was then closing, and the results of the sowing are most definite: not all the good seed sown comes to fruitage, or wheat, and the wheat and the tares grow *together* until the end of the age. This interpretation is not fanciful, for it is given by Christ Himself; and the parables which follow must necessarily agree with these. The third and fourth are of the mustard seed and the measure of meal. Though commonly interpreted to mean the worldwide development of the church and the permeating influence of the Gospel, in the light of the interpretation of the previous parables they can mean only the mixture of evil with that which began as small as a mustard seed and as pure as meal. No one can reasonably deny the fact that even the true believers have been influenced by that which leaven represents according to the Bible. The "leaven of the Pharisees" is formalism; the "leaven of the Sadducees" is rationalism; and "the leaven of the Herodians" is worldliness. The fifth parable is of a treasure hid in a field, which pictures the earthly people in the world, while their real relation to Christ is covered until the accomplishment of that which is revealed in the sixth. Here the same man, the Lord Jesus Christ, sells all that He hath to purchase the Church, the pearl of great price, for He "loved the church, and gave himself for it" (Eph. 5:25); the pearl, by its formation and its power to reflect the light, is a wonderful type of the Church in her present formation and future place in glory. Both the treasure and the pearl are found in the world, but do not include all of the world. The last parable but restates the truth that the mixture of the good and the evil is to continue to the end of the age.

The highest ambition of the great missionary, Paul, was to be all things to all men that he might save *some*, not *all*. He found that his preaching was a savour of "death unto death" as well as of "life unto life" (2 Cor. 2:15, 16), and he clearly states in 2 Timothy 3:13, "But evil men and seducers shall wax worse and worse, deceiving, and being deceived." Christ also predicted that the end of this age should be marked by such sin as provoked the judgment of the flood: "But as the days of Noe were, so shall also the coming of the Son of man be. For as in the days that were before the flood they were eating and drinking, marrying and giving in marriage, until the day that Noe entered into the ark, and knew not until the flood came, and took them all away; so shall also the coming of the Son of man be" (Matt. 24:37-39).

This truth is often rejected as being pessimistic and disloyal to the progress of the world, yet has not the history of the age verified the teaching. And is not the coming glory nearer and more certain when depending upon His promised return in resistless power and splendor, than when depending upon any human progress the world has ever known? One is the majestic movement of the divine program in fulfillment of every covenant while the other is the vain dream of the world in its ignorance and disregard for the testimony of God.

Because of the presence of these two classes in the world during this age, there are two very distinct lines of scripture descriptive of them. One body of scripture directly applies to and governs the "wheat" or heavenly people, and one applies to the "tares," the "children of the evil one." The marvelous revelation of the believer's relation to Christ and the heavenlies, and his deliverance from any actual identification with this age, though in it, will be the subject of another chapter. Only the relation of the unregenerate to this world and to Satan will be considered at this point.

As it has pleased Satan to hide himself and all his projects from the unbelieving world, that which God has revealed in all faithfulness will be received only by those who have unquestioning confidence in His Word.

According to the Scriptures, the relation of the unbelieving to Satan is far more vital than a mere pleasure-seeking allegiance. On two occasions Jesus spoke of the unsaved as the "children of Satan" (Matt. 13:38; John 8:44), and Paul so addressed Elymas, the sorcerer, according to Acts 13:10. The same class is also twice called the "children of disobedience" (Eph. 2:2; Col. 3:6), and once it is called the "children of wrath" (Eph. 2:3).

It is evident that these are descriptions of the same class of people, since both terms are employed together in Ephesians 5:6: "Let no man deceive you with vain words: for because of these things cometh the wrath of God upon the children of disobedience." The exact cause of that wrath is stated in Romans 1:18 (R.V.) "For the wrath of God is revealed from heaven against all ungodliness and unrighteousness of men, who hinder the truth in unrighteousness." Therefore, the willful neglect and disregard of the testimony of God by the world has allied them with Satan, and placed them under the wrath of God, which must find its righteous execution in due time if grace is not accepted.

Again, Satan is revealed as directing and empowering the children of disobedience: "And you hath he quickened, who were dead in trespasses and sins; wherein in time past ye walked according to the course of this world [*age*], according to the prince of the power of the air, the spirit that now worketh in the children of disobedience" (Eph. 2:1, 2). The real force of this passage, also, is dependent upon the meaning of one word; the word "worketh" being the same as is used in Philippians 2:13, where God is said to impart His wisdom and strength to the believer: "For it is God which worketh in you both to will and to do of his good pleasure." Additional light may be had as to the reality of this relationship and the impartation of power which it implies from the following passages in which the same Greek word is used. (The word in question is here italicized): "And there are diversities of operations, but it is the same God that *worketh* all in all" (1 Cor. 12:6); "But all these [gifts] *worketh* that one and the selfsame Spirit, dividing to every man several-ly as he will" (1 Cor. 12:11); "And what is the exceeding great-ness of his power to us-ward who believe, according to the working of his mighty power, which he *wrought* in Christ when he raised him from the dead, and set him at his own right hand in the heavenlies" (Eph. 1:19-20); "For he that *wrought effectually* in Peter to the apostleship of the circumcision, the same was *mighty* in me toward the Gentiles" (Gal. 2:8); "Whereunto I also labor, striving according to his working, which *worketh* in me mightily" (Col. 1:29); "Now unto him that is able to do exceed-ing abundantly above all that we ask or think, according to his power that *worketh* in us" (Eph. 3:20). It is also said in regard to the energizing power of Satan, using the same Greek word: "For the mystery of iniquity doth already *work*" (2 Thess. 2:7); "For when we were in the flesh, the motions of sins, which were by the law, did *work* in our members to bring forth fruit unto death" (Rom. 7:5). In the last two passages quoted, the meaning is, like the preceding passages, of an imparted energy, and is, therefore, most suggestive.

It may then be concluded from the testimony of the Scrip-

tures that Satan imparts His wisdom and strength to the unbelieving in the same manner the power of God is imparted to
the believer by the Holy Spirit. There is, however, no revelation
as to the comparative degree of strength imparted by each. It
should be further noted in this connection that this impartation
of energizing power from Satan is not toward a limited few
who might be said, because of some strange conduct, to be
possessed of a demon; but is the common condition of all who
are yet unsaved, and are, therefore, still in the "power of darkness."

The relation between the unregenerate and Satan is still more
vital, according to the Greek text from which 1 John 5:19 is
translated. The Authorized Version renders it, with marginal
note, as follows: "We know that we are of God, and the whole
world lieth in the evil one." In this passage there are two star-
tling revelations in regard to this relationship. First, the word
"in" is the same as is used everywhere of the believer when he
is said to be *in* Christ, and in the case of the believer it signifies
an organic union to Christ. As a branch is *in* the vine, so the believer is *in* Christ. Though the word, when used of the unregenerate, cannot mean the same degree of organic
life-relationship as exists between Christ and the believer, yet it
does denote a deep relationship; and Satan is the light, inspira-
tion, and power, of all those whom he energizes.

The second revelation in the passage is found in the word
"lieth" —"The whole world lieth in the evil one." It might
possibly be translated "lieth asleep," for its condition is not
only a fixed position in the evil one, but is also a condition of
unconsciousness. The saved ones are said to be in the Father's
hand where no created thing can pluck them out (John 10:29),
and underneath are the everlasting arms: so the great mass of
unsaved humanity are in the arms of Satan, and by his subtlety
they are all unconscious of their position and relation. This is
not at all strange. Even the believer has no present power to
discern his glorious position and security in the Father's hand,
apart from the assurance of the written Word. Much less, then,
can the unbeliever come to realize his own position in the arms
of Satan, when, under the direction of Satan, he gives no heed
to the testimony of God.

Still another passage should be noted in this connection. In 2 Cor. 4:3, 4, Satan is described as the god of this world, blinding the minds of the unbelieving. The whole passage is as follows: "And if our gospel is veiled, it is veiled in them that perish: in whom the god of this age hath blinded the thoughts of the unbelieving that the light of the gospel of the glory of Christ, who is the image of God should not dawn upon them" (R.V. with margin). In this passage the unconscious condition is said to be the direct result of the power of Satan, and the blindness of their thoughts, it is stated, is along one particular line. To them the *gospel* is veiled; and the gospel here referred to is not the whole life story of Jesus, nor is it the "Gospel of the kingdom"; but the message of good news or favor—the exact terms of salvation by grace alone. This Paul here calls "my gospel," for to him it was first unfolded in its completeness.

The unregenerate are, then, unconscious of their position in the arms of Satan, and blind in their thoughts toward the gospel of mercy and grace— their only hope for time or eternity. Satan, like a fond mother, is bending over those in his arms, breathing into their minds the quieting balm of a "universal fatherhood of God" and a "universal brotherhood of man," suggesting their worthiness before God on the ground of their own moral character and physical generation; feeding their tendency to imitate the true faith by great humanitarian undertakings and schemes for the reformation of individuals and the betterment of the social order. God's necessary requirements of regeneration are carefully set aside, and the blinded souls go on without hope, "having the understanding darkened, being alienated from the life of God through the ignorance that is in them, because of the blindness of their heart" (Eph. 4:18). How important, as a preparation for salvation, is the illuminating work of the Spirit in conviction, by which He lifts the veil and opens the mind to a new vision of the redemption and glory that is in Christ! Without this God-given vision there can be no understanding of the way of life, nor any intelligent decision for Christ.[1]

---

1. The divine part in the salvation of men is more fully presented in the author's book, *True Evangelism*.

4

This Age and the Satanic System

It may also be concluded from the study of the ages that God has not been pleased to meet the presumptuous claims of Satan or of man by a simple denial of those claims; He has chosen rather to bring everything to an experimental test. One advantage of this method is obvious: every mouth will be stopped, and the entire universe of beings will see clearly the utter folly of that which might have been arbitrarily denied. Man can no longer claim that his conscience is sufficient to guide him to his highest destiny; since the whole race, when standing on that basis before God, so utterly failed that their destruction by a flood was necessary. In like manner, by the history of a most favored people in the age preceding the first advent of Christ, man has demonstrated his own inability to do right or to keep the law. In the present age, man proves his separation from his Creator by his spirit of self-sufficiency and positive rejection of God. The present issue between God and man is one of whether man will accept God's estimate of him, abandon his hopeless self-struggle, and cast himself only on the grace of God which alone is sufficient to accomplish his needed transformation.

All divine love, wisdom, and power have wrought to provide salvation for man; and when this last and supreme effort of God has been rejected, the final pleading with man must be forever past, and the long delayed judgment upon sin be executed in righteousness.

It has already been pointed out that Satan purposed in his

heart to attempt all the functions of God; and, according to the Scriptures, that which he purposed is being permitted, to the extent of his ability, throughout the course of this age. Though his failure and defeat have been predicted from the beginning, it has pleased God to permit the Satanic ambition to come to its own destruction, and to demonstrate its own weakness and wicked folly. No other solution is given of the present power of Satan and the manifestations of his increasing authority yet to be experienced in the closing scenes of this age.

His present authority is by no means complete. In 2 Thessalonians 2:7 (R.V.) it is stated: "The mystery of lawlessness doth already work: only there is one that restraineth now, until he be taken out of the way." This is believed to be a description of the work of the Holy Spirit as He restrains and hinders the development of the power of evil. Nor can Satan direct the affairs of that part of humanity who have been delivered from the power of darkness and are now united to Christ (unless they yield to his wishes), though they are in the world and their earth lives are mingled in much of its history. These saved ones are the antiseptic salt, hindering, like the Spirit who indwells them, the untimely dissolution of humanity. Again, Satan's dominion is limited in that "there is no power but of God: the powers that be are ordained of God" (Rom. 13:1). In this scripture it is revealed that Satan, though in authority, is not wholly free from his Creator, and that any direction of the governments of the world which he exercises is by permission from God. Therefore, the efforts of Satan and man are not supreme, but must come to their predicted end when the eternal purpose of God has had its realization in the gathering out from both Jews and Gentiles a heavenly people for His own name.

The whole race but recently trembled and suffered under the untold agony of a world-war, and yet there are still those who are confident that the sagacity of man is not only controlling iniquity, but is gradually developing an improved social order. Thus, man, in his vanity, assigns to himself that which is of God alone, for all the elements of corruption and tribulation are latent in the world today, and the mighty effort of God is required to stay its bursting into flame until the appointed time.

Tribulation will, therefore, instantly begin when the hand of God is removed from the unregenerate and Satan-ruled humanity.

Though under the restraining hand of God, Satan, according to the Scriptures, is now in authority over the unregenerate world, and the unsaved are unconsciously organized and federated under his leading. The fact that there is such a federation, although stated in the Bible, is obscured in translation. In at least thirty important passages the English word "world" is again used without qualification. In these passages reference is made to a great evil system or order over which Satan is in authority, the word "world" referring to the world of men, their evil undertakings, ideals and federation. This federation includes all of the unsaved and fallen humanity; it has the cooperation of the fallen spirits, and is the union of all who are living and acting in independence of God. This Satanic system has its own ideals and principles which are in sharp contrast to the ideals and principles given to the redeemed, yet these two classes must mingle together as closely as the ties of human life can bring them.

The whole truth concerning this federation is contained in those passages wherein the Satanic system is mentioned.

First, *Satan is its governing head*. Three times Jesus referred to Satan as the prince of the Satanic system: "Now is the judgment of this world: now shall the prince of this world [Satanic system] be cast out" (John 12:31). "Hereafter I will not talk much with you: for the prince of this world [*Satanic system*] cometh, and hath nothing in me" (John 14:30). "Of judgment, because the prince of this world [*Satanic system*] is judged" (John 16:11). Paul also refers to Satan as the "prince of the power of the air" (Eph. 2:2), and again as the "god of this world [*age*]" (2 Cor. 4:4). In the latter passage, mention is made of the age or period of time only, as in Ephesians 6:12: "For our wrestling is not against flesh and blood, but against the principalities, against the powers, against the age rulers of this darkness, against the spiritual hosts of wickedness in the heavenlies" (R.V.).

An important revelation regarding the present authority of Satan over the world is given in the letter to the church in Pergamos. The ascended Lord said to this church: "I know thy works, and where thou dwellest, even where Satan's seat [throne] is." The church at Pergamos, being in the world, was under the fierce attack of the one whose rule is over the earth.

From these scriptures it must be conceded that the offer, which Satan made to Christ, of the then inhabited earth, was very real. The scripture is as follows: "And the devil, taking him up into an high mountain, showed him the kingdoms of the world in a moment of time. And the devil said unto him, All this power will I give thee, and the glory of them: for that is delivered unto me; and to whomsoever I will I give it. If thou therefore wilt worship me, all shall be thine" (Luke 4:5-7). It has sometimes been held that the claim of possession of the kingdoms of the world was a lie, this being asserted on the ground that Satan is exposed in the Scriptures as a liar. Such a conclusion is impossible for at least two reasons. The offer would have had no value had he not possessed the kingdoms he offered; and any such false claim would have been immediately branded as a lie by the Son of God. In two additional passages, Satan is still further revealed as the recognized head of this world-system: "Because greater is he that is in you than he that is in the world [*Satanic system*]" (1 John 4:4). "And we know that we are of God, and the whole world [*Satanic system*] lieth in the wicked one" (1 John 5:19).

Returning to Isaiah 14:12-19, wherein Satan is described as "Lucifer, the son of the morning," and where the prophet in vision sees the whole career of Satan in retrospect, it will be seen that Satan holds a mighty grip upon the world. Here it is said of him that he was the one who "didst weaken the nations" and who "made the earth to tremble, that did shake kingdoms, that made the world as a wilderness, and destroyed the cities thereof; that opened not the house of his prisoners." Every phrase in this remarkable passage is a revelation. Probably there is reference here both to the fall of man and to the authority of Satan in the earth, as well as to his attitude of resistance toward salvation which is by the grace of God, since it is said of Satan that he "made the world as a wilderness; he opened not the house of his prisoners."

Second, *the Satanic system, according to the Scriptures, is wholly evil*. This is a hard saying, and is usually denied by those who do not realize that all scripture estimates are made from the standard of the holiness of God, and that the Satanic system, of itself and apart from the influence of God and His people, has never improved their own moral condition, but that they are individually under condemnation before God (John 3:18), their borrowed interest in morality and charity being a poor commendation, in view of their fallen and Christ-rejecting attitude before God. They are also incapable of comprehending the standards of God, whose thoughts and ways are above their thoughts and ways as the heavens are higher than the earth (Isa. 55:8, 9). The quality and incapacity of the fallen race is accurately described in Romans 3:10-18, this description of them being as they appear before the holiness of God, stripped of all externals: "As it is written, There is none righteous, no, not one: there is none that understandeth, there is none that seeketh after God. They are all gone out of the way, they are together become unprofitable; there is none that doeth good, no, not one. Their throat is an open sepulchre; with their tongues they have used deceit; the poison of asps is under their lips: whose mouth is full of cursing and bitterness: their feet are swift to shed blood: destruction and misery are in their ways: and the way of peace have they not known: there is no fear of God before their eyes." So, fallen humanity federated under Satan will appear and act when the restraining hand of God is removed. Though the unsaved are moral, educated, refined, or religious, they are not *righteous* in God's sight; for the charge here brought against them is that "there is none righteous, no, not one"; and *all* "have sinned and come short of the glory of God."

The following scriptures which directly refer to the character of the Satanic system are, therefore, the estimate of God upon those conditions which the world holds to be ideal. "Whereby are given unto us exceeding great and precious promises: that by these ye might be partakers of the divine nature, having escaped the corruption that is in the world [*Satanic system*]" (2 Pet. 1:4). "For if after they have escaped the pollutions of the world [*Satanic system*] through the knowledge of the Lord and Saviour Jesus Christ, they are again entangled therein, and overcome, the latter end is worse with them than the beginning"

(2 Pet. 2:20). "Pure religion and undefiled before God and the Father is this, To visit the fatherless and widows in their affliction, and to keep himself unspotted from the world [*Satanic system*]" (Jas. 1:27). "Ye adulterers and adulteresses, know ye not that the friendship of the world [*Satanic system*] is enmity with God? Whosoever therefore will be a friend of the world [*Satanic system*] is the enemy of God" (Jas. 4:4). "For whatsoever is born of God overcometh the world [*Satanic system*]" (1 John 5:4). "Hereafter I will not talk much with you: for the prince of this world [*Satanic system*] cometh, and hath nothing in me" (John 14:30). "And every spirit that confesseth not that Jesus Christ is come in the flesh is not of God: and this is that spirit of antichrist, whereof ye have heard that it should come; and even now already is it in the world [*Satanic system*]" (1 John 4:3). In like manner the believer is said to have been "delivered from the present evil age" (Gal. 1:4), and "delivered from the power of darkness" (Col. 1:13), and is not to be conformed to this age (Rom. 12:2).

These judgments are made from the viewpoint of the purity and holiness of God. In His sight the highest moral, educational, and religious ideals that the unregenerate world can comprehend are but a part of the confusion and darkness of this age when coupled with a rejection of His testimony in regard to His Son as their atoning Savior.

Thus, it is presented from the scriptures that the present age and its great federation is, in God's sight, most unholy.

Third, *Satan is also set forth as having direct control of the physical well-being of his subjects, and at the same time as being able, by special permission, to gain access to the people of God:* "Forasmuch then as the children are partakers of flesh and blood, he [Christ] also himself likewise took part of the same; that through death he might destroy him that had the power of death, that is, the devil" (Heb. 2:14). "How God anointed Jesus of Nazareth with the Holy Ghost and with power: who went about doing good, and healing all them that were oppressed of the devil; for God was with him" (Acts 10:38). "And ought not this woman, being a daughter of Abraham, whom Satan hath bound, lo, these eighteen years, be loosed from this bond on the Sabbath day?" (Luke 13:16). "Then Satan answered the Lord, and said, Doth

Job fear God for naught! Hast not thou made an hedge about him, and about his house, and about all that he hath on every side! Thou hast blessed the work of his hands, and his substance is increased in the land. But put forth thine hand now, and touch all that he hath, and he will curse thee to thy face. And the Lord said unto Satan, Behold, all that he hath is in thy power; only upon himself put not forth thine hand" (Job 1:9-12). "Simon, Simon, behold, Satan asked to have you, that he might sift you as wheat: but I have made supplication for thee, that thy faith fail not; and do thou, when once thou hast turned again, establish thy brethren" (Luke 22:31, 32, A.V.). "And lest I should be exalted above measure through the abundance of the revelations, there was given to me a thorn in the flesh, the messenger of Satan to buffet me, lest I should be exalted above measure" (2 Cor. 12:7).

By these passages, the emphasis of the scriptures on the power and authority of Satan in this age may be seen. And though the exact limits of his power under the restraining hand of God are not revealed, it would be unreasonable to deny that he is the god of this age, the head of the great world system; and, though all unknown to them, the director of the affairs of unregenerate men.

Fourth, *the works of the Satanic order are clearly outlined in several descriptive passages which also present that which is highest in ideal, and deepest in motive in the Satan-energized mass of humanity.* One passage, alone, contains the entire revelation: "For all that is in the world [*Satanic system*], the lust of the flesh, and the lust of the eyes, and the pride of life, is not of the Father, but is of the world [*Satanic system*]" (1 John 2:16). The satisfaction of these same cravings was the temptation placed before Eve in the Garden: "And when the woman saw that the tree was good for food, and that it was pleasant to the eyes, and a tree to be desired to make one wise, she took of the fruit thereof, and did eat and gave also unto her husband with her; and he did eat" (Gen. 3:6). The real nature of these cravings is easily recognized as being wholly self-centered and without thought of God.

All "wars and fightings" among men are only a natural result of the evil qualities of this great federation. Jesus said to Pilate: "My kingdom is not of this world [*Satanic system*]: if my kingdom were of this world [*Satanic system*], then would my servants fight, that I should not be delivered unto the Jews: but now is my kingdom not from hence" (John 18:36). It is a noticeable fact that the governments of the world depend upon physical power and a display of armament to maintain their position and authority, and the superior law of love is not adapted to, or understood by, the elements that make up the Satanic order.

Fifth, *all earthly property is of the Satanic order, which property the believer may use, but must not abuse:* "But whoso hath this world's good [*Satanic system*], and seeth his brother have need, and shutteth up his bowels of compassion from him, how dwelleth the love of God in him?" (1 John 3:17). "And the cares of this world [*age*], and the deceitfulness of riches, and the lust of other things entering in, choke the word, and it becometh unfruitful" (Mark 4:19). "But this I say, brethren, the time is short: it remaineth, that both they that have wives be as though they had none; and they that weep, as though they wept not; and they that rejoice, as though they rejoiced not; and those that buy, as though they possessed not; and they that use this world [*Satanic system*], as not abusing it" (1 Cor. 7:29-31).

Sixth, *the same world that crucified the Christ will also hate the saved one in whom He dwells:* "Marvel not, my brethren, if the world [*Satanic system*] hate you" (1 John 3:13).

Seventh, *the impotency and limitations of the world-order are most evident.* Its leader, though mighty, is inferior to Christ: "Ye are of God, little children, and have overcome them: because greater is he that is in you, than he that is in the world [*Satanic system*]" (1 John 4:4). Its knowledge and understanding are limited: "Behold what manner of love the Father hath bestowed upon us, that we should be called children of God; and such we are. For this cause the world [*Satanic system*] knoweth us not, because it knew him not" (1 John 3:1, R.V.). "Now the natural man receiveth not the things of the Spirit of God: for they are foolishness unto him; and he cannot know them, because they are spiritually judged. But he that is spiritual judgeth all things, and he himself is judged of no man" (1 Cor. 2:14, 15, R.V.).

"There is none that understandeth, there is none that seeketh after God" (Rom. 3:11). "And even if our gospel is veiled, it is veiled in them that perish: in whom the god of this age hath blinded the minds of the unbelieving, that the light of the gospel of the glory of Christ, who is the image of God, should not dawn upon them" (2 Cor. 4:3, 4, A.V.). "They are of this world [*Satanic system*]: therefore speak they as of the world, and the world [*Satanic system*] heareth them" (1 John 4:5, R.V.). All the sorrow of this order is without hope: "For godly sorrow worketh repentance unto salvation, a repentance which bringeth no regret: But the sorrow of the world [*Satanic system*) worketh death" (2 Cor. 7:10, R.V.). And, finally, the whole order is temporal and passing: "But the day of the Lord will come as a thief in the night; in the which the heavens shall pass away with a great noise, and the elements shall melt with fervent heat, and the earth also and the works that are therein shall be burned up" (2 Pet. 3:10). "And the world [*Satanic system*] passeth away and the lust thereof: but he that doeth the will of God abideth forever" (1 John 2:17).

5

The Satanic Host

In one of His controversies with the Pharisees (Matt. 12:22-30) Christ inferred that Satan is a king, and as such is in authority over a kingdom (see also Rev. 2:13, A.V.). This particular discussion was in regard to the fact that Christ had healed one "possessed with a demon, blind and dumb." The Pharisees claimed that the demon had been cast out by Beelzebub the prince of demons, or by the one whom Jesus, later in the narrative, calls Satan. The passage is as follows: "Then was brought unto him one possessed with a devil, blind, and dumb; and he healed him, insomuch that the blind and dumb both spake and saw. And all the people were amazed, and said, Is not this the son of David! But when the Pharisees heard it, they said, This fellow doth not cast out devils, but by Beelzebub the prince of the devils. And Jesus knew their thoughts, and said unto them, Every kingdom divided against itself is brought to desolation; and every city or house divided against itself shall not stand: and if Satan cast out Satan, he is divided against himself; how shall then his kingdom stand! And if I by Beelzebub cast out devils, by whom do your children cast them out! Therefore they shall be your judges. But if I cast out devils by the Spirit of God, then the kingdom of God has come unto you. Or else how can one enter into a strong man's house, and spoil his goods, except he first bind the strong man! And then he will spoil his house. He that is not with me is against me; and he that gathereth not with me scattereth abroad."

By this scripture it may be seen that a portion of the kingdom of Satan is a host of bodiless spirits. Although their origin cannot be definitely traced, it is probable that they were created as subjects of Satan in the primal glory, as he, also, was created as their prince and king. Satan, being in authority over these beings, doubtless drew them after him in his sinful attempt to thrust himself into the place of God.

Long before man was created, sin began with "Lucifer, the son of the morning," and extended to a multitude of angels concerning whom it is said that they "kept not their first estate;" and, "God spared not the angels that sinned, but cast them down to hell, and delivered them into chains of darkness, to be reserved unto judgment" (John 8:44; 2 Peter 2:4; Jude 6). Another company of fallen angels became demons and are still free to serve in the projects of Satan.

It would seem that Satan is in authority over two distinct orders of beings—the Satanic order of the earth, and the Satanic host of the air. It is clear that he secured the scepter of government in the earth from Adam, by right of conquest: while His authority over the Satanic host is undoubtedly that which he has been permitted to retain from his creation. If Satan has thus kept his authority over these spirits from the beginning, it follows that they are in full sympathy with him and render him willing service. The following scriptures emphasize the authority of Satan over these beings: "And if Satan cast out Satan, how then shall his kingdom stand?" (Matt. 12:26). "Then shall he say also unto them on the left hand, Depart from me, ye cursed, into everlasting fire, prepared for the devil and his angels" (Matt. 25:41).

The reality and personality of this host of evil spirits is taught in the Bible, and a careful study of the numerous passages in which they are mentioned will reveal how God has provided complete instruction in His Word concerning the facts and forces which constantly confront the believer.

These spirits are usually referred to in both the Authorized and Revised Versions of the New Testament as "devils," but the word might better have been translated "demons."

In considering the service these beings render to Satan, it is important to distinguish between demon possession or control, and demon influence. In the one case the body is entered and a dominating control is gaited: while in the other case a warfare from without is carried on by suggestion, temptation, and influence.

Investigation of the scriptures in regard to demon possession reveals:

First, *that this host is made up of bodiless spirits only.* The following scriptures verify this statement: "When the unclean spirit is gone out of a man, he walketh through dry places, seeking rest, and findeth none. Then he saith, I will return into my house from whence I came out; and when he is come, he findeth it empty, swept, and garnished. Then goeth he, and taketh with himself seven other spirits more wicked than himself, and they enter in and dwell there: and the last state of that man is worse than the first" (Matt. 12:43-45). "And all the devils besought him, saying, Send us into the swine, that we may enter into them" (Mark 5:12).

Second: *they are, however, not only seeking to enter the bodies of either mortals or beasts, for their power seems to be in some measure dependent upon such embodiment; but they are constantly seen to be thus embodied, according to the New Testament.* A few of these passages are given here: "When the even was come, they brought unto him many that were possessed with devils: and he cast out the spirits with his word, and healed all that were sick" (Matt. 8:16). "As they went out, behold, they brought to him a dumb man possessed with a devil. And when the devil was cast out, the dumb spake" (Matt. 9:32, 33). "And the people with one accord gave heed unto those things which Philip spake, hearing and seeing the miracles which he did. For unclean spirits, crying with loud voice, came out of many that were possessed with them: and many taken with palsies, and that were lame, were healed" (Acts 8:6, 7). "And it came to pass, as we went to prayer, a certain damsel possessed with a spirit of divination met us, which brought her masters much gain by soothsaying" (Acts 16:16). "And they came over unto the other side of the sea, into the country of the Gadarenes. And when he was come out of the ship, immediately there met him out of the tombs, a man with an unclean spirit, who had his dwelling among the tombs; and no man could bind him, no, not with chains: because that he had been often bound with fetters and chains, and the chains had been plucked asunder by him, and the fetters broken in pieces: neither could any man tame him. And always, night and day, he was in the mountains, and in the tombs, crying, and cutting himself with stones. But when he saw Jesus afar off, he ran and worshipped him, and cried with a loud voice, and said, What have I to do with thee, Jesus, thou Son of the most high God! I adjure thee by God, that thou torment me not. For he said unto him, Come out of the man, thou unclean spirit. And he asked him, What is thy name! And he answered, saying, My name is Legion: for we are many. And he besought him much that he would not send them away out of the country. Now there was nigh unto the mountains a great herd of swine feeding. And all the devils besought him, saying, send us into the swine, that we may enter into them. And forthwith Jesus gave them leave. And the unclean spirits went out, and entered into the swine: and the herd ran violently down a steep place into the sea, (they were about two thousand;) and were choked in the sea" (Mark 5:1-13).

Third, *they are wicked, unclean, and vicious*. Many passages might be quoted in proof of this statement. "And when he was come to the other side into the country of the Gergesenes, there met him two possessed with devils, coming out of the tombs, exceeding fierce, so that no man might pass by that way" (Matt. 8:28). "And when he had called unto him his twelve disciples, he gave them power against unclean spirits, to cast them out, and to heal all manner of sickness and all manner of disease" (Matt. 10:1). "There met him out of the tombs a man with an unclean spirit, who had his dwelling among the tombs; and no man could bind him, no, not with chains: because that he had been often bound with fetters and chains, and the chains had been plucked asunder by him, and the fetters broken in pieces: neither could any man tame him. And always, night and day, he was in the mountains, and in the tombs, crying, and cutting himself with stones" (Mark 5:2-5). "And they brought him unto him: and when he saw him, straightway the spirit tare him; and he fell on the ground, and wallowed foaming" (Mark 9:20).

It might be added that there seem to be degrees of wickedness represented by these spirits: for it is stated in Matthew

12:43-45 that the demon, returning to his house, "taketh with himself seven other spirits more wicked than himself."

The question is often raised whether demon possession obtains at the present time. Although the authentic records of such control are almost wholly limited to the three years of the public ministry of Jesus, it is incredible that demon possession did not exist before that time, or has not existed since. In this connection it should be remembered that these beings are not only intelligent themselves, but that they are directly governed and ordered by Satan, whose wisdom and cunning are so clearly set forth in the Scriptures. It is reasonable to conclude that they, like their monarch, are adapting the manner of their activity to the enlightenment of the age and locality. It is evident that they are not now less inclined than before to enter and dominate a body. Demon possession in the present time is probably often unsuspected because of the generally unrecognized fact that demons are capable of inspiring a moral and exemplary life, as well as of appearing as the dominating spirit of a spiritist medium, or through the grosser manifestations that are recorded by missionaries concerning conditions which they observe in heathen lands. These demons, too, like their king, will appear as "angels of light" as well as "roaring lions," when by the former impersonation they can more perfectly further the stupendous undertakings of Satan in his warfare against the work of God.

Demon influence, like the activity of Satan, is prompted by two motives: both to hinder the purpose of God for humanity, and to extend the authority of Satan. They, therefore, at the command of their king, willingly cooperate in all his God dishonoring undertakings. Their influence is exercised both to mislead the unsaved and to wage an unceasing warfare against the believer (Eph. 6:12).

Their motive is suggested in what is revealed by their knowledge of the authority and deity of Christ, as well as by what they know of their eternal doom. The following passages are important in this connection: "And behold, they cried out, saying, What have we to do with thee, Jesus, thou Son of God! Art thou come hither to torment us before the time?" (Matt. 8:29). "And there was in their synagogue a man with an unclean spirit; and he cried out, saying, Let us alone; what have we to do with thee, thou Jesus of Nazareth? Art thou come to destroy us! I know thee who thou art, the Holy One of God. And Jesus rebuked him, saying, Hold thy peace, and come out of him" (Mark 1:23-25). "And the evil spirit answered and said, Jesus I know, and Paul I know; but who are ye?" (Acts 19:15). "Thou believest that there is one God; thou doest well: the devils also believe, and tremble" (Jas. 2:19).

Of the methods of demons in the latter days of the age, the Scriptures bear special testimony. They will cover their lies with the empty form of religion, and by every means make them to appear as the truth, that they may rob both the saved and the unsaved of their hope in Christ: "Now the Spirit speaketh expressly, that in the latter times some shall depart from the faith, giving heed to seducing spirits, and doctrines of devils; speaking lies in hypocrisy; having their conscience seared with a hot iron" (1 Tim. 4:1, 2). A departure from the true faith is thus predicted to be the evidence of the influence of demons in the last days. This is not a reference to an individual Christian turning from his own personal faith. It is none other than the great apostasy that must precede the "Day of the Lord" according to 2 Thessalonians 2:2, 3.

The believer's victory in this unceasing warfare is treated at length in another chapter. It may be noted here, however, that the Lord said to His followers, "Howbeit this kind goeth not out but by prayer and fasting" (Matt. 17:21) but since the beginning of this dispensation, which is characterized by the presence of the Spirit in every believer, the victory is through the power of the indwelling Spirit: "Because greater is he that is in you, than he that is in the world" (1 John 4:4). Such is the whole armor of God: "Wherefore take unto you the whole armour of God, that ye may be able to withstand in the evil day, and having done all, to stand" (Eph. 6:13).

Satan, though proposing to supersede the Almighty, is not Omnipotent; but his power and the extent of his activity are immeasurably increased by the co-operation of his host of demons. Satan is not Omniscient; yet his knowledge is greatly extended by the combined wisdom and observation of his sympathetic subjects. Satan is not Omnipresent; but he is able to keep up an unceasing activity in every locality by the loyal obedience of the Satanic host, who are so numerous as to be called "Legion."

6

Satan's Motive

According to the Scriptures, the supreme motive of Satan is his purpose to become like the Most High and, though that purpose was formed even before the age of man, it has been his constant actuating motive from that time until now. It is also the teaching of the scriptures that Satan is in especial authority in the present age, he being permitted the exercise of his own power in order that he, and all his followers, may make their own final demonstration to the whole universe of the utter folly of their claims and of their abject helplessness when wholly independent of their Creator. This is definitely predicted in 2 Timothy 3:9 as the final outcome of the attitude of the world in its independence toward God: "They shall proceed no further: for their folly shall be manifest unto all men."

It has also been stated that the unsurpassed tribulation only awaits the withdrawal of the restraining hand of God, for all the required elements for such a condition are latent in the unregenerate heart (Rom. 3:9-18). In this period of tribulation the greatest power of Satan will be exercised, and the wickedness of man will be revealed in his attempt to live in complete separation from God.

Even fallen humanity would not, at first, acknowledge Satan as its object of worship and federal head; and such a condition of society wherein Satan will be received as supreme, as he will be in the person of the first Beast of Revelation 13, must, therefore, be developed by increasing irreverence and lawlessness toward God. Thus it has been necessary for Satan to conceal his person and projects from the very people over whom he is in authority and in whom he is the energizing power. For this reason this class of humanity believes least in his reality, and ignorantly rejects its real leader as being a mythical person. When he is worshiped, it is through some idol as a medium, or through his own impersonation of Jehovah; and when he rules, it is by what seems to be the voice of a king, or the voice of the people. However, the appalling irreverence of the world today is the sure preparation for the forthcoming direct manifestation of Satan, as predicted in Daniel 9; 2 Thessalonians 2; and Revelation 13.

Satan's policy of deception is described as extending to all the nations, and to the whole world: "Even him, whose coming is after the working of Satan with all power and signs and lying wonders, and with all deceivableness of unrighteousness in them that perish; because they received not the love of the truth, that they might be saved" (2 Thess. 2:9, 10). "And the great dragon was cast out, that old serpent, called the Devil, and Satan, which deceiveth the whole world" (Rev. 12:9). "And he laid hold on the dragon, that old serpent, which is the Devil, and Satan, and bound him a thousand years, and cast him into the bottomless pit, and shut him up, and set a seal upon him, that he should deceive the nations no more till the thousand years should be fulfilled: and after that he must be loosed a little season" (Rev. 20:2, 3). "And when the thousand years are expired, Satan shall be loosed out of his prison, and shall go out to deceive the nations which are in the four quarters of the earth" (Rev. 20:7, 8). He who was the measure of perfection, full of beauty and wisdom, he who made the earth to tremble, who shook kingdoms, has been willing to be ridiculed by the world as a being without reality, that he might in the end realize his own deepest desire.

Again, his own subjects have strangely neglected the plain teachings of scripture concerning his real power and authority. To them he has been an imaginary fiend, delighting only in the torment of unfortunate souls, making his home in hell, and himself the impersonation of all that is cruel and vile: when, on the contrary, he is real, and is the very embodiment of the highest ideals that the unregenerate world has received, for he is the inspirer of all those ideals. With his own he is not at enmity, and he, like the most refined of the world, is not in sympathy with the grosser forms of their sin. He would hinder those manifestations of evil if he could. And certainly he does not prompt them, for they are the natural fruit of an unrestrained fallen nature, according to James 1:14, 15: "But every man is tempted, when he is drawn away of his own lust, and enticed. Then when lust hath conceived, it bringeth forth sin: and sin, when it is finished, bringeth forth death." "For from within, out of the heart of men, proceed evil thoughts, adulteries, fornications, murders, thefts, covetousness, wickedness, deceit, lasciviousness, an evil eye, blasphemy, pride, foolishness: all these evil things come from within, and defile the man" (Matt. 7:21-23). The dying drunkard, the fallen woman, and the suffering of the innocent are more likely the evidences of Satan's failure rather than the realization of his purpose.

His own terrible sin before God would not be condemned in the eyes of the world, for it is that which they most idealize and praise. In his sin he aspired to that which is highest, and proposed to realize his ideal by his own self-sufficiency and strength. True, he has lowered his Creator, in his own mind, to a level where he supposes himself to be in legitimate competition with Him, both for authority over other beings and for their worship. Yet this unholy ambition and disregard for the Creator is a most commendable thing according to the standards of the Satanic order. In the language of the world, Satan is simply "self made" and every element of his attitude toward his Creator is, as a principle of life, both commended and practiced by the world.

Though hiding himself, Satan has had the satisfaction, under limitations, of governing the affairs of men; and the delight, to a large extent, of receiving their worship. The greatest care was taken in the law governing God's ancient people that they should not offer their sacrifices unto devils, which was the practice of surrounding nations (Lev. 17:7; Deut. 32:17). In violation of these special laws, Rehoboam instituted special priests for the devils (2 Chron. 11:15), while the worship of devils, according to the New Testament, is to continue throughout the age: "But this I say, that the things which the Gentiles sacrifice, they sacrifice to devils, and not to God: and I would not that ye should have fellowship with devils. Ye cannot drink the cup of the Lord, and the cup of devils: ye cannot be partakers of the Lord's table and the table of devils" (1 Cor. 10:20, 21). "And the rest of the men that were not killed by these plagues yet repented not of the works of their hands, that they should not worship devils, and idols of gold, and silver, and brass, and stone, and of wood: which neither can see, nor hear, nor walk" (Rev. 9:20).

Again Satan's ambition is leading him to make this age of his special opportunity as nearly perfect as his wisdom and power will permit. And in this connection it may be noted that Satan's ambition was not to become a fiend, but rather to become like the Most High. He will, therefore, strive for all that is moral and good: yet at the same time do all in his power to draw men from their natural reverence of God, in order that, in due time, they may acknowledge himself without fear. The Satanic ideal of this age is, then, an improved social order, a moral and cultured people who are devout worshipers of himself, though for the present they may imagine that they are worshiping Jehovah through their empty religious forms and ceremonies, while they are really in a state of God-dishonoring unbelief, and all their thoughts are energized by Satan alone. The Satanic message for this age will be reformation and self-development, while the message of God is regeneration by the power of the Spirit.

Satan, in his imitation of the Most High, is also working toward a universal kingdom of morality and peace upon earth, which will be temporarily realized under the reign of the Beast (Rev. 13). The difference between Satan's ideal and the purpose of God, apart from the utter folly of the one and the glorious certainty of the other, is the difference of both method and time. According to the Satanic program, the present order of society, with Satan on the throne, is to be developed into an ideal brotherhood, in which all men will practice that which is moral and good. According to the Word of God, this is an evil age of darkness and pollution, in which the folly of Satan and man is to be proven, and out of which God is to gather the heavenly people for His own name. The kingdom of righteousness is then to follow, being ushered in by Christ-enthroning and Satan-dethroning events. There will then be a perfect humanity and social order for all shall know the Lord from the least unto the greatest and righteousness and peace shall cover the earth as the waters cover the face of the deep.

The master passion of Satan leads him, not only to strive for the success of his own projects, but also to wage an unceasing warfare against Jehovah. These two lines of activity are inseparable; for he cannot establish and develop his own kingdom, and at the same time permit his subjects to be translated out of his kingdom into another, especially when they remain in the midst as a living power and testimony against him. Nor can he reasonably allow the accomplishment of any of the projects of God, for it is predicted that at the completion of these his own doom will be at hand. The present time is, therefore, to Satan the time of struggle for his own existence, as well as for the realization of all that has been his ambition in the ages past. The warfare is no mere passing amusement for him, for he, in desperation, is facing a terrible judgment if he cannot succeed in his purpose.

The spectacle now presented to the universe is that of a mighty celestial being, the god of the earth, who is by creation the full measure of perfection both in wisdom and beauty, making his last and most desperate warfare, not only to realize his own ambition but also to thwart every movement of the Most High; knowing that in failure there is no ground for mercy, but only the final destruction that has been so long predicted. He knew when he formed this God-dishonoring purpose that it must either wholly succeed or he himself fall into eternal judgment. On the other side of the conflict there is perfect calmness and certainty as to the end, for the judgment and sentence are past; yet every true believer is implored to be instant in season and out of season in the present projects of grace, that the sufferings and separations of earth may be cut short in righteousness.

Well may believers study their own motives in service in view of these vastly differing programs; and question whether there is in them a humble willingness to cooperate in the present purpose of God in preparing the Bride for the returning King.

Or whether, on the other hand, they have carelessly fallen in with the Satanic ideal which rejects the coming kingdom of Christ by an unholy attempt to establish the present kingdom of Satan.

The program of Satan, which the world calls "optimistic," rests on the Satanic purpose of a reformed society: in contrast, the program of God, which is called "pessimistic," in that it discredits this age, rests upon the infinite wisdom, love and power of God, and is so certain and near that the believer is taught to watch, wait, and be ready for the first divine movement toward this glorious end.

The motive of Satan is four times revealed, and these disclosures stand out like milestones in his career.

First, his master passion is given in the record of his first sin. His secret purpose, it is stated, was to be "like the Most High" (Isa. 14:14).

Second, when he met the first Adam in the Garden and there recommended his own unholy ideal in the words, "Ye shall be as gods" (Gen. 3:5).

Third, when he met the Last Adam in the wilderness he again manifests his desire to take the place of God. Well he knew that Christ is very God; yet he said to Him, "If thou wilt worship me" (Luke 4:7).

Fourth, his motive is finally revealed in the assumption of the Man of Sin of whom it is predicted that he "as God sitteth in the temple of God, setting himself forth as God" (2 Thess. 2:4, R.V.).

7

Satan's Methods

The two great activities of Satan, already mentioned, are referred to in 2 Thessalonians 2:4, in connection with the Man of Sin who will be Satan's last and greatest manifestation. This being is spoken of as he "who opposeth and exalteth himself above all that is called God, or that is worshipped." These two activities are inseparable in that, while Satan is seeking to exalt himself above all that is called God or that is worshipped, he can keep his subjects or prolong his own existence only by an unceasing warfare in which he opposes himself against God. Whether Satan now believes that he may yet succeed in spite of the decree of the cross and the evident superior power of God, is not revealed.

It is still further disclosed that the enmity of Satan is not only toward the person of God from whom he has everything to fear, but also toward every true child of God. Too much emphasis cannot be placed on this fact. Satan has no controversy or warfare with his own unregenerate people, but there is abundant scripture to prove that he makes unceasing effort to mar the life and service of believers. The motive for this effort is all-sufficient: they have "partaken of the divine nature" (2 Pet. 1:4), and afford, therefore, a possible opportunity for Satan to thrust his fiery darts at the divine Person. Thus the believer becomes a medium of connection between the divine Person and the Satanic order, for God literally loves the unsaved through the believer (Rom. 5:5) and on the other hand, the prince of the Satanic system, as well as many of his subjects, is seeking an opportunity for a thrust through the believer at the person of God. Several important passages on the latter point may here be noted: "These things have I spoken unto you, that in me ye might have peace. In the world ye shall have tribulation: but be of good cheer; I have overcome the world" (John 16:33). "Yea, and all that will live godly in Christ Jesus shall suffer persecution" (2 Tim. 3:12). "Marvel not, my brethren, if the world hate you" (1 John 3:13). "Casting all your care upon him; for he careth for you. Be sober, be vigilant; because your adversary the devil, as a roaring lion, walketh about, seeking whom he may devour: whom resist steadfast in the faith, knowing that the same afflictions are accomplished in your brethren that are in the world" (1 Pet. 5:7-9). "Finally, my brethren, be strong in the Lord, and in the power of his might. Put on the whole armour of God, that ye may be able to stand against the wiles [literally, artifices] of the devil. For our wrestling is not against flesh and blood, but against the principalities, against the powers, against the world rulers of this darkness, against the spiritual hosts of wickedness in the heavenly places" (Eph. 6:10-12, R.V.).

The teaching of these passages clearly indicates the Satanic enmity toward the believer, and the believer's . . . utter helplessness apart from the divine sufficiency. They also reveal a degree of enmity which would result in the believer's life being crushed out, were it not for the evident answer to the prayer of Jesus: "I pray not that thou shouldest take them from the world, but that thou shouldest keep them from the evil one" (John 17:15, R.V.). Certainly there is abundant reason for the believer to expect the fiercest opposition from Satan and his host in all his life and service, and faith alone insures his victory over the world.

The believer is also the object of the Satanic attack because of the fact that unto the child of God is committed the great ministry of reconciliation; that by his testimony both in life and word, and by his prayers, the facts of redemption may be given to the world. If Satan can cripple the believer's service he accomplishes much in resisting the present purpose of God. No other explanation is adequate for the dark pages of church history, the appalling failure of the church in world-wide evangelism, or her present sectarian divisions and selfish indifference.

This blighting Satanic opposition may be detected in every effort for the salvation of the lost. It may be seen in the fact that no personal appeal is ever made to the vast majority even in this favored land; moreover, when an appeal is made, it is easily distracted or diverted into the discussion of unimportant themes. The faithful pastor or evangelist is most sorely assailed, every device of Satan being used to distort the one all-important message of grace into something which is not vital. The evangelist's call for decisions is often cumbered with that which is misleading or is a positive misstatement of the terms of salvation; thus the appeal is lost and the whole effort fails. The action of Satan may also be detected in the fact that a humble messenger who is loyal to Christ and His salvation by grace alone, will be almost unheeded at the present time: while the vast throng will be found supporting that which is religious only in its externals, but which is in reality a gospel of morality and is a subtle denial of the redemption that is in Christ.

Again, the opposing power of Satan may be seen in the matter of Christian giving. Millions are given without solicitation for education, culture, and humanity's physical comfort, but real worldwide evangelization must ever drag on with its shameful limitations and debts. This warfare of Satan is even more noticeable in the believer's prayer life. This, being his place of greatest usefulness and power, is subject to the severest conflict. In this connection it may be stated safely that there is comparatively but little prevailing prayer today, yet the way is open and the promises are sure. If the believer cannot be beguiled into indifference or a denial of Christ, he is often tempted to place an undue emphasis upon some minor truth, and, in partial blindness, to sacrifice his whole influence for good through the apparent unbalance of his testimony.

Satan's warfare against the purpose of God is still more evident in his direct hindering of the unsaved. Not only are they constantly blinded to the Gospel, but, when the Spirit would draw them, their minds are often filled with strange fears and distorted visions. Their inability to cast themselves upon Christ is a mystery to themselves, and nothing but the direct illuminating power of the Spirit in conviction can open their eyes and deliver them from their gross darkness.

Satan has always adapted his methods to the times and conditions. If attention has been gained, a complete denial of the truth has been made; or, when some recognition of the truth is demanded, it has been granted on the condition that that which is vital in redemption should be omitted.

This partial recognition of the truth is required by the world today. For, while the direct result of the believer's testimony to the Satanic system has been toward the gathering out of the Bride, there has been an indirect influence of this testimony upon the world which has led them to see that all that is good in their own ideals has been already stated in the Bible and exemplified in the life of Jesus. Moreover, they have heard that every principle of humanitarian sympathy or righteous government has been revealed in the scriptures of Truth. Thus there has grown a more or less popular appreciation of the value of these moral precepts of the scriptures and of the example of Christ. This condition has prevailed to such a degree that any new system or doctrine which secures a hearing today must base its claim upon the Bible, and include, to some extent, the Person and teachings of Jesus. The fact that the world has thus partly acknowledged the value of the Scriptures is taken by many to be a glorious victory for God; while, on the contrary, fallen humanity is less inclined to accept God's terms of salvation than in the generations past.

It is evident that this partial concession of the world to the testimony of God has opened the way for counterfeit systems of truth, which, according to prophecy, are the last and most to be dreaded methods in the Satanic warfare. In this connection it must be conceded that Satan has really granted nothing from his own position, even though he be forced to acknowledge every principle of truth save that upon which salvation depends. Rather is he advantaged by such a concession; for the value and delusion of a counterfeit is increased by the nearness of its likeness to the real. By advocating much truth, in the form of a counterfeit system of truth, Satan can satisfy all the external religious cravings of the world, and yet accomplish his own end by withholding that on which man's only hope depends. It is, therefore, no longer safe to subscribe blindly to that which promises general good, simply because it is good and is garnished with the teachings of the Bible; for good has ceased to be all on one side and evil all on the other. In fact, that which is evil in purpose has gradually appropriated the good until but one issue distinguishes them. Part-truth-ism has come into final conflict with whole-truth-ism, and woe to the soul that does not discern between them. The first, though externally religious, is of Satan, and leaves its followers in the doom of everlasting banishment from the presence of God: while the latter is of God, "having promise for the life that now is and that which is to come."

It is also noticeable that the term "infidel" has, within a generation, disappeared from common usage, and that manner of open denial of the truth has been almost wholly abandoned. Yet the real Church has by no means lost her foes, for they are now even more numerous, subtle, and terrible than ever before. These present enemies, however, like the unclean birds in the mustard tree, have taken shelter under her branches. They are officiating at her most sacred altars and conducting her institutions. These vultures are fed by a multitude, both in the church and out, who, in Satanic blindness, are committed to the furtherance of any project or the acceptance of any theory that promises good to the world or is apparently based upon scripture, little realizing that they are often really supporting the enemy of God.

A counterfeit is Satan's most natural method of resisting the purpose of God, since by it he can realize to that extent his desire to be *like* the Most High. Every material is now at hand, as never before, for the setting up of those conditions which are predicted to appear only in the very end of the age. In 2 Timothy 3:1-5 one of these predictions may be found: "This know also, that in the last days perilous times shall come. For men shall be lovers of their own selves, covetous, boasters, proud, blasphemers, disobedient to parents, unthankful, unholy, without natural affection, truce-breakers, false accusers, incontinent, fierce, despisers of those that are good, traitors, heady, high-minded, lovers of pleasures more than lovers of God; having a form of godliness, but denying the power thereof: from such turn away."

Every word of this prophecy is worthy of most careful study

in the light of the present tendency of society. The fifth verse is especially important in connection with the subject of counterfeits of the truth: "Having a form of godliness, but denying the power thereof: from such turn away."

Here it is stated that in these last days forms of godliness shall appear which, however, deny the power of God; and from such the believer is warned to turn away. The important element in the true faith which is to be omitted in these "forms" is carefully defined elsewhere in the Scriptures: "For I am not ashamed of the gospel of Christ: for it is the power of God unto salvation to every one that believeth; to the Jew first, and also to the Greek" (Rom. 1:16). "But we preach Christ crucified, unto the Jews a stumbling-block, and unto the Greeks foolishness; but unto them which are called, both Jews and Greeks, Christ the power of God, and the wisdom of God" (1 Cor. 1:23, 24). Therefore, that which is omitted so carefully from these forms is the salvation which is in Christ. This is most suggestive, for "there is none other name under heaven given among men, whereby we must be saved," and it is by salvation alone that any deliverance can be had from the power of darkness. Without this salvation Satan can still claim all his own. It is perhaps necessary to add that, judging from all his writings, this salvation of which Paul confesses he was not ashamed was no less an undertaking than regeneration by the Spirit; and whatever other theories may be advanced, this is the teaching of the Spirit through the apostle Paul.

This prophecy concerning conditions in the "last days" ends with an injunction which is addressed only to the believers who are called upon to live and witness during those days. To them it is said: "from such [forms of godliness which deny the power thereof] turn away." As certainly as the "last days" are now present, so certainly this injunction is now to be heeded, and the Lord's people are called upon to separate from churches and institutions which deny the Gospel of God's saving grace through the substitutionary blood redemption of the cross. To support institutions or ministries which "deny the power thereof," is to lend aid to Satan—the enemy of God.

It therefore follows that one feature of the last days will be a form of godliness which carefully denies the power of God in salvation.

Again, Satan is "in the latter times" to be the promoter of a system of truth or doctrine: "Now the Spirit speaketh expressly, that in the latter times some shall depart from the faith, giving heed to seducing spirits, and doctrines of devils; speaking lies in hypocrisy; having their conscience seared with a hot iron" (1 Tim. 4:1, 2). These predicted Satanic systems are here carefully described. Their offers will be so attractive and externally so religious that into them will be drawn some "who shall depart from the faith"; they being enticed by seducing spirits. These attractive systems are not only from Satan, but are themselves "lies in hypocrisy," being presented by those whose conscience has been seared with a hot iron. No more illuminating terms could be used than these. A lie covered by hypocrisy means, evidently, that they are still attempting to be counted among the faithful; and the conscience seared would indicate that they can distort the testimony of God and blindly point other souls to the bottomless pit, without present remorse or regret.

The doctrine of devils is again referred to in Revelation 2:24 as "the deep things of Satan," and this is Satan's counterfeit of "the deep things of God" which the Spirit reveals to them that love Him (1 Cor. 2:10).

Thus there are predicted for the last days of this age, both a form of godliness which denies the power of salvation that is in Christ, and a system known as "the deep things of Satan" or "doctrines of devils," speaking lies in hypocrisy. Can there be any doubt that these two scriptures describe the same thing, since they also refer to the same time? The lies of one can be but the covered denial of salvation in the other.

Again, Satan has his assembly or congregational meeting which is his counterfeit of the visible church. This assembly is referred to, both in Revelation 2:9 and 3:9, as the "synagogue of Satan;" an organized assembly being relatively as important for the testimony in the deep things of Satan as it has been in the things of God.

In Matthew 13 the tares appear *among* the wheat and their appearance is said to be after the sowing of the wheat. So, also, the "children of the wicked one" appear and are often included and even organized within the forms of the visible church.

The assembly of Satan, calling itself a part of the visible church, is to have its ministers and teachers. This is stated in 2 Corinthians 11:13-15: "For such are false apostles, deceitful workers, transforming themselves into the apostles of Christ. And no marvel; for Satan himself is transformed into an angel of light. Therefore it is no great thing if his ministers also be transformed as the ministers of righteousness; whose end shall be according to their works." Here is a remarkable revelation of the possible extent of the Satanic counterfeit: "False apostles, deceitful workers, transforming themselves into apostles of Christ" and "ministers of righteousness;" yet these are shown to be only agents of the great deceiver, Satan, who is himself transformed into an angel of light. It is evident that the method of this deception is to imitate the real ministers of Christ.

Certainly these false apostles cannot so appear unless they gather into their message every available "form of godliness" and cover their lies with the most subtle hypocrisy. Evil will not appear on the outside of these systems; but they will be announced as "another gospel" or as a larger understanding of the previously accepted truth, and will be all the more attractive and delusive since they are heralded by those who claim to be ministers of Christ, who reflect the beauty of an "angel of light," and whose lives are undoubtedly free from great temptation. It should be noted, however, that these false ministers do not necessarily know the real mission they have. Being unregenerate persons of the Satanic system, and thus blinded to the real Gospel, they are sincere, preaching and teaching the best things the angel of light, their energizing power, is pleased to reveal unto them. Their gospel is one of human reason, and appeals to human resources. There can be no appreciation of divine revelation in them, for they have not come really to know God or His Son, Jesus Christ. They are ministers of righteousness which should never be confused with the preaching of grace. One is directed only at the reformation of the natural man, while the other aims at regeneration through the power of God. As all this is true, how perilous is the attitude of many who follow attractive ministers and religious guides only because they claim to be such and are sincere, and who are not awake to the one final test of doctrine by which alone the whole covered system of Satanic lies may be distinguished from the truth of God. In this connection John writes the following warning: "If there come any unto you, and bring not this doctrine, receive him not into your house, neither bid him God speed" (2 John 10).

False teachers are usually sincere and full of humanitarian zeal; but they are unregenerate. This judgment necessarily follows when it is understood that they deny the only ground of redemption. Being unregenerate, it is said of them: "But the natural man receiveth not the things of the Spirit of God: for they are foolishness unto him: neither can he know them, because they are spiritually discerned" (1 Cor. 2:14). Such religious leaders may be highly educated and able to speak with authority on every aspect of human knowledge, but if they are not born again, their judgment in spiritual matters is worthless and misleading. All teachers are to be judged by their attitude toward the doctrine of the blood redemption of Christ, rather than by their winsome personalities, or by their sincerity.

There yet remains one mighty element in the program of Satan's counterfeits in addition to his outward forms, deep doctrines, church and ministers—that is, the Man of Sin, the blasphemous counterfeit of the blessed Christ; who is yet to appear; who will be the very incarnation of Satan; and "whose coming is after the working of Satan with all power and signs and lying wonders and all deceivableness of unrighteousness in them that perish" (2 Thess. 2:9, 10). As the whole purpose of God in the ages has its consummation in the yet future coming of Christ, so Satan, in imitation of the program of God, has appointed a coming one (2 Thess. 2:9), who will be his greatest manifestation, and upon whom he will bestow his greatest wisdom, power and attractiveness. The study of this mighty and imposing character can only be suggested in the following pages.

The titles of Satan would indicate that he is attempting, also, in himself to counterfeit the Persons of the blessed Trinity. He appears as "the god of this world" in imitation of God the Father; he appears as the "prince of the world" in imitation of God the Son; and "the spirit that now energizeth in the children of disobedience" is his imitation of God the Spirit who dwells in and energizes the true believers. Thus his desire to be like the Most High has led him to a blasphemous attempt to imitate all the separate manifestations of the three Persons of the Godhead. But since redemption, which he proposes to hinder, is the work of the second Person—God the Son—Satan more often appears as a counterfeit of Christ, both in title and undertaking; and this is the character in which he makes his last and most desperate effort before he is banished to the pit and his final judgment is begun.

8

The Man of Sin

Reference has already been made to a period of tribulation yet to come upon the earth. That period is referred to in the Bible by various figures: "The great tribulation," "the time of Jacob's trouble," and "a day of darkness and gloominess, a day of clouds and thick darkness." It is also described as the culmination of the great apostasy, which apostasy is predicted for the end of this age, and which is emphasized in the later Epistles of the New Testament. These Epistles not only recognize a complete apostasy yet to come in this age, but teach that the germ of that apostasy was apparent even then at the time when they were written. This teaching of the apostles finds its natural culmination in the last book of the Bible wherein the exact development of the apostasy and the conditions to prevail in the tribulation are recorded at length. All other references, both in the Old Testament and the New, perfectly agree with this extended description.

In reference to the time of the tribulation which is thus predicted, Paul states in 2 Thessalonians 2:3: "Let no man deceive you by any means: for that day ['the day of the Lord'] shall not come, except there come a falling away first, and that man of sin be revealed, the son of perdition," thus showing that the tribulation precedes the Day of the Lord. In Revelation 19, that day is seen to be the termination of the tribulation, which is previously described in that book. This period of tribulation is, therefore, to come before the kingdom age, and to be ended by the glorious appearing of Christ, the King.

79

Again, the tribulation is to come after the true Church has been removed; for it should be remembered that the true believers are to be saved out of the "hour of trial which shall come upon the earth to try those that dwell therein" (Rev. 3 10), and he is not "appointed unto wrath" (1 Thess. 5:9). The believer, being a citizen of heaven is, therefore, not included among those who dwell in the earth. The Lord comes first, not to the earth, but into the air to meet His Bride and gather her to Himself; both those that are sleeping and those that are awake: "For the Lord himself shall descend from heaven with a shout, with the voice of the archangel, and with the trump of God: and the dead in Christ shall rise first: then we which are alive and remain shall be caught up together with them in the clouds, to meet the Lord in the air: and so shall we ever be with the Lord" (1 Thess. 4:16, 17). His coming to receive His heavenly people—the Church—is imminent and has been since the promises of His return were given; and it is for this particular preliminary event that the Church is taught to hope and pray, for it will be the time of her rapture and blessedness. As has been before stated, the utter dissolution of humanity is latent in the unregenerated heart (Rom. 3:10-18), and its own tribulation only awaits this removal of all divine restraint. It is, therefore, both scriptural and reasonable to conclude that tribulation will instantly begin upon the earth after Christ comes *for* His Church.

Thus it may be seen that this period of unsurpassed trial upon the earth, when the blasphemous claims of Satan and man are to be proven and God's testimony is to be vindicated, is bounded by the two events: when He comes *for* His saints (1 Thess. 4:16, 17), to gather to Himself His heavenly people, and when He comes *with* His saints (Rev. 19:11-21), at which time He will completely fulfil all the covenants of God with His earthly people.

The actual duration of this period is marked off in Daniel 9:24-27: "Seventy weeks are determined upon thy people and upon thy holy city, to finish the transgression, and to make an end of sins, and to make reconciliation for iniquity, and to bring in everlasting righteousness, and to seal up the vision and prophecy, and to anoint the most Holy. Know therefore and understand, that from the going forth of the commandment to restore and to build Jerusalem unto the Messiah the Prince shall be seven weeks, and three score and two weeks: the street shall be built again, and the wall, even in troublous times. And after the three score and two weeks shall Messiah be cut off, but not for Himself: and the people of the prince that shall come shall destroy the city and the sanctuary; and the end thereof shall be with a flood, and unto the end of the war desolations are determined. And he shall confirm the covenant with many for one week: and in the midst of the week he shall cause the sacrifice and the oblation to cease, and for the overspreading of abominations he shall make it desolate, even until the consummation, and that determined shall be poured upon the desolate."

There are three distinct periods of time here indicated. First, seventy weeks (the Hebrew word refers to a period which may be divided into seven, whether days, weeks, or years) between the time of the vision and the age of "everlasting righteousness" and anointing of the most Holy; or, from the time of the vision to the earthly kingdom of Christ, which is yet future. Second, sixty-nine weeks, beginning to reckon from the same time, or from the command of the King of Babylon to restore Jerusalem, and continuing unto the death of Christ which is referred to as the "cutting off of the Messiah." And lastly, one week, for the overspreading of abomination and that which is determined to be poured upon the desolate.

History fortunately interprets the time here indicated: for, from the command of the King to rebuild Jerusalem, to the death of Christ was 483 years, or sixty-nine weeks of seven years each. This leaves but the one additional week of the seventy before the bringing in of the everlasting righteousness. That one week is here described as the time of most terrible desolation and overspreading of abomination when the people are under a covenant with another prince. This present age is as a parenthesis in Jewish history and, as no account is made of it in these reckonings, the last unfulfilled week (seven years) of the seventy, before the kingdom is established upon the earth, must be the time between the gathering out of the Church—an event which completes the purpose of this parenthetical age—and the final bringing in of the kingdom.

The last period of seven years of desolation is, however, to be shortened, according to the words of Christ: "For then shall be great tribulation, such as was not since the beginning of the world to this time, no, nor ever shall be. And except those days should be shortened, there should no flesh be saved: but for the elect's sake those days shall be shortened" (Matt. 24:21, 22). It should be noticed that this period cannot be confused easily with any other, for it is referred to as the time more terrible than any other that has ever been, or ever will be (Dan. 12:1; Joel 2:2; Matt. 24:21, 22).

Reference has been made at length to the tribulation period in order to make clear the exact conditions in which the Man of Sin is to appear; for this mighty world ruler makes his advent in those days of earth's darkness and gloom when all the light of God has been withdrawn, and the world is left in its own helpless confusion. He appears in the tribulation as the agent of Satan after that mighty head of the Satanic system has been cast out of heaven into the earth (Rev. 12:7-12). The time of the destruction of the Man of Sin is also revealed in that it is mentioned as one of the events in the glorious coming of Christ (Dan. 2:44; 7:11-14; 2 Thess. 2:8; Rev. 19:20). He, therefore, appears as the culmination of the Satanic effort, and a careful study of his person and character will reveal the fact that he is the most stupendous work of Satan in his enmity against God.

In connection with the time of the Man of Sin, it is also to be noted that the believer is not directly warned against his person, but is, rather, warned against the conditions that are to prevail as a preparation for his coming. This is due to the fact that the true believers are to be gathered to their Lord before that "wicked one" appears, and they are, therefore, only in danger of being influenced by that which precedes and prepares for his coming. His description is set forth at length only in such passages as deal with the whole and final development of the age.

It should also be remembered that the description of this person, like that of the person and work of Satan, is from the standpoint of the holiness of God; and that which the world will hail as its glorious ideal of perfection is, in God's sight, the personification of rebelliousness, blasphemy, and treason.

The order of the governments and rulers of the world in this Gentile age is revealed to Daniel in visions which are recorded and interpreted in the book of Daniel. In these visions the Man of Sin appears as the "little horn" of Daniel 7 and is the last and most God-dishonoring world-ruler. He also later appears as the "desolator" of Daniel 9:27; the "willful king" of Daniel 11:36; the "abomination of desolation" of Matthew 24:15; the "man of sin" of 2 Thessalonians 2; the rider on the white horse of Revelation 6:2; and the first Beast of Revelation 13. His identity is certain, even though he appears under various figures and titles; for he, like Satan, is so unique in his character, time, and undertakings, that he cannot he confused easily with any other.

In Daniel 2 the order of Gentile governments is set forth by the figure of the great image which, at the last, is suddenly and violently shattered by the "stone cut from the mountain without hands:" which stone is Christ, the Corner Stone; and the Stone which the builders rejected. The feet and toes of this image are said to be the last manifestation of human government, and it is this part of the image that is violently shattered by the stone. Of this termination of earthly rule it is recorded in Daniel 2:44, 45: "And in the days of these kings shall the God of heaven set up a kingdom, which shall never be destroyed: and the kingdom shall not be left to other people, but it shall break in pieces and consume all these kingdoms, and it shall stand forever. For as much as thou sawest that the stone was cut out of the mountain without hands, and that it brake in pieces the iron, the brass, the clay, the silver, and the gold; the great God hath made known to the king what shall come to pass hereafter; and the dream is certain, and the interpretation thereof sure."

From this chapter it may be seen that the setting up of the Messianic Kingdom is to be both sudden and destructive to all human governments, and that it is in no way the result of an age of development and progressive improvement.

In Daniel 7 the Man of Sin appears, as has been stated, as the "little horn" among ten horns, which, like the ten toes of the great image, indicate the extreme end of human authority and power. In this vision the latter end of the kingdoms of the earth is seen to culminate in the one most daring ruler, the "little horn," who has "a mouth speaking great things" and whose look is more imposing than all others; and he it is who makes war with the saints and prevails over them until the coming of the Ancient of Days. The inspired interpretation of the vision is given in Daniel 7:23-27: "Thus he said, the fourth beast shall be the fourth kingdom upon earth, which shall be diverse from all kingdoms, and shall devour the whole earth, and shall tread it down, and break it in pieces. And the ten horns out of this kingdom are ten kings that shall arise: and another shall arise after them; and he shall be diverse from the first, and he shall subdue three kings. And he shall speak great words against the most High, and shall wear out the saints of the most High, and think to change times and laws: and they shall be given into his hand until a time and times and the dividing of time. But the judgment shall sit, and they shall take away his dominion, to consume and destroy it unto the end. And the kingdom and dominion, and the greatness of the kingdom under the whole heaven, shall be given to the people of the saints of the most High, whose kingdom is an everlasting kingdom, and all dominion shall serve and obey him."

In Daniel 11 the reign of the Man of Sin, the willful king, is prophesied in detail; and the fact is stated that the reign and the blasphemous attitude of this last great ruler are both in the purpose of God. A portion of this remarkable passage is here given: "And the king shall do according to his will; and he shall exalt himself, and magnify himself above every God, and shall speak marvellous things against the God of gods, and shall prosper until the indignation be accomplished: for that is determined shall be done. Neither shall he regard the God of his fathers, nor the desire of women, nor regard any god: for he shall magnify himself above all. But in his estate shall he honor the God of forces: and a god whom his fathers knew not shall he honor with gold, and silver, and with precious stones, and pleasant things. Thus shall he do in the most strong holds with a strange god, whom he shall acknowledge and increase with glory: and he shall cause them to rule over many, and shall divide the land for gain." This last verse is more clearly translated "and he will practice in the strongholds of fortresses with a strange god; whoso acknowledgeth him will be increased with glory; and he shall cause them to rule over the many, and shall divide the land to them for a reward" (Dan. 11:36-39).

In addition to disregard for God on the part of the Man of Sin, this passage presents several important revelations. First, the expression "the God of his fathers" would seem to indicate that the Man of Sin would come from a lineage of God-fearing people. Second, his disregard for the desire of women is possibly a result of his hatred of the true Messiah; for this reference may be to the desire of every Jewish woman to be the mother of Messiah. Third, those who acknowledge the strange god (Satan), whom he honors, will be prospered, and the land will be divided unto them and he will give them authority and glory.

In the New Testament the Man of Sin is described as "the one who comes in his own name," whom men will receive (John 5:43); "that man of sin," "the son of perdition" (2 Thess. 2:3); "that Wicked" (one) (2 Thess. 2:8) and the "beast" (Rev. 13:1), and to him Satan gives all the power and glory which he offered to Christ (Luke 4:5, 6). Of the many references to him, two passages deal with him at length. In the first (2 Thess. 2:1-10), his coming is mentioned as directly following the removal of God's present restraint from the earth; and in the second (Rev. 13:1-8), as before stated, his coming is seen directly to follow the casting of Satan from heaven into the earth (Rev. 12:7-12), and continues until the glorious appearing of Christ, which is described in Rev. 19 and 20.

The former passage (2 Thess. 2:1-10) is as follows: "Now, we beseech you, brethren, by the coming of our Lord Jesus Christ, and by our gathering together unto him, that ye be not soon shaken in mind, or be troubled, neither by spirit, nor by word, nor by letter as from us, as that the day of Christ [the Lord] is at hand. Let no man deceive you by any means: for that day shall not come, except there come a falling away first, and that man of sin be revealed, the son of perdition; who opposeth and exalteth himself above all that is called God, or that is worshipped; so that he as God sitteth in the temple of God, shewing himself that he is God. Remember ye not, that, when I was yet with you, I told you these things? And, now, ye know what withholdeth that he might be revealed in his time. For the mystery of iniquity doth already work: only he who now letteth [restrains] will let, until he be taken out of the way. And then shall that Wicked [one] be revealed, whom the Lord shall consume with the spirit of his mouth, and shall destroy with the brightness of his coming; even him, whose coming is after the working of Satan with all power and signs and lying wonders, and with all deceivableness of unrighteousness in them that perish; because they receive not the love of the truth, that they might be saved."

In this passage it is predicted of this mighty person that he will assume to be very God, "sitting in the temple as God," and winning the worship of the multitude by his miraculous power, signs, and lying wonders; deceiving all who perish, and who would not receive the love of the truth that they might be saved.

Still another and more striking description of this person is given in the second passage just mentioned (Rev. 13:1-8): "And I stood upon the sand of the sea, and saw a beast rise up out of the sea, having seven heads and ten horns, and upon his horns ten crowns, and upon his heads the name of blasphemy. And the beast which I saw was like unto a leopard, and his feet were as the feet of a bear, and his mouth as the mouth of a lion: and the dragon [Satan] gave him his power, and his seat, and his great authority. And I saw one of his heads as it were wounded to death; and his deadly wound was healed: and all the world wondered after the beast. And they worshipped the dragon [Satan] which gave power unto the beast; and they worshipped the beast, saying, Who is like unto the beast? Who is able to make war with him? And there was given unto him a mouth speaking great things and blasphemies; and power was given unto him to continue forty and two months. And he opened his mouth in blasphemy against God, to blaspheme his name, and his tabernacle, and them that dwell in heaven. And it was given unto him to make war with the saints, and to overcome them: and power was given him over all kindreds, and tongues, and nations. And all that dwell upon the earth shall worship him, whose names are not written in the book of life of the Lamb slain from the foundation of the world."

The first and, it would seem, most important thing that is stated of this being in this scripture is that one of his heads was, as it were, wounded to death, and his deadly wound was healed.

Some have claimed this to be a reference to a previous political defeat followed by reinstatement into power. This may be included, but the expression is, however, most suggestive and significant as an attempt on the part of Satan to imitate, in the Man of Sin, that which was the supreme miracle of the Christ— His death and resurrection. The effort is plainly effective; more so than a mere shifting of political fortune could possibly be, for the statement follows, "All the world wondered after the beast who had received the deadly wound and yet lived." After they wondered, they worshipped. First they worshiped Satan, who performed the mighty miracle; and then they worshiped the beast, saying, "Who is like unto the beast? Who is able to make war with him?" The blasphemy of the Man of Sin has been emphasized in all scripture references to him, and is here still more vividly pictured.

The time he is to continue is said to be forty and two months, which would be one-half the tribulation period; and this statement is probably not at all figurative. By his overwhelming supernatural power and wisdom he gains authority over every individual in the Satanic system (excepting those recorded in the Lamb's book of life). These are not brought under his governing power.

The latter part of the chapter presents still another mighty person, who is also called a "beast," but later appears as the false prophet (Rev. 19:20) and who exercises all the power of the first beast, and receives his power from the dragon, Satan. Much is said of this second "beast," but his mission is in no way to attract attention to himself. He cooperates in gaining world-wide worship and authority for the first beast, whose deadly wound was healed. The second beast seems to deal directly with the people and by his mighty signs and miracles, as well as by his authority, he compels loyalty to the first beast. Fire is called down from heaven, and a dumb idol is made to speak and live. He is able to establish a union of all people in trade, imposing a death penalty upon them. And by all these means he furthers the interests of the first beast. The scripture here referred to is as follows: "And I beheld another beast coming up out of the earth; and he had two horns like a lamb, and he spake as a dragon [Satan]. And he exerciseth all the power of the first beast before him, and causeth the earth and them which dwell therein to worship the first beast, whose deadly wound was healed. And he doeth great wonders, so that he maketh fire come down from heaven on the earth in the sight of men, and deceiveth them that dwell on the earth, by the means of those miracles which he had power to do in the sight of the beast; saying to them that dwell on the earth, that they should make an image to the beast, which had the wound by a sword, and did live. And he had power to give life unto the image of the beast, that the image of the beast should both speak, and cause so that as many as would not worship the image of the beast should be killed. And he causeth all, both small and great, rich and poor, free and bond, to receive a mark in their right hand, or in their foreheads: and that no man might buy or sell, save he that had the mark, or the name of the beast, or the number of his name. Here is wisdom. Let him that hath understanding count the number of the beast: for it is the number of a man; and his number is Six hundred three score and six" (Rev. 13:11-18).

There is a deep suggestion in the person of this second beast of a counterfeit of the Holy Spirit of God, He who came not to speak from Himself, but to glorify Christ and to unite all believers, leading them in worship and praise. This second beast is probably identical with "Antichrist" who appears under that title only in the writings of John, and who is there seen as the consummation of a long succession of false religious teachers who have denied the Christ and His sacrificial work.

When the testimony of all the scriptures relating to the Man of Sin is considered, he is seen to be a person whose superhuman power is plainly ascribed to Satan. He appears upon the scene, after the removal of the heavenly people and during the great tribulation, as the climax of all Satanic exaltation and opposition to God. He is the last and greatest of earthly rulers, and, from his position of unsurpassed influence, speaks great words and manifests great wisdom. He is externally religious, and the promoter of righteous projects and principles which in God's sight are only hypocrisy and blasphemy because of the subtle Christ-denying motive which prompts all his undertakings. His hold upon the public mind is by a process which is natural. Great miracles are performed by himself and by his prophet —fire is called down from heaven, a dumb idol is made to speak and live, and he himself has been wounded to death and yet lives. By such supernatural works his assumption to be very God is accepted, and he becomes the world's ideal of all that is supreme. The people are said first to marvel and wonder; then to worship at his feet; and at last, in mad devotion, they challenge the universe to produce his equal—"Who is like the beast?" they cry. He has been wounded to death and yet lives; he performs as great miracles as the world has ever seen; and he must, therefore, be God manifest in the flesh. His wisdom, beauty and majesty are a seeming warrant for the highest adoration.

Thus the Man of Sin will appear as the culmination of all the counterfeit methods of Satan, which methods had their beginnings in the last days of the age, even before the calling away of the true Church, the Body of Christ. The subtle doctrines of devils will be adopted as creeds in assemblies and so-called churches, and these deep things, with the Satanic ambition for moral improvement, will be voiced by ministers who appear as apostles of Christ and ministers of righteousness. Yet in God's sight it is all a deep lie and hypocrisy, for they are distorting His truth and subtly denying His redemption.

All this, as has been stated, is but the Satanic preparation of humanity that they may wholly acknowledge Satan as their god, and that he may himself become like the Most High. This program is permitted in the purpose of God, for "that is determined shall be done" (Dan. 11:36). It will be only for a moment; for the resistless coming of the "Ancient of Days" will unveil all this deception, banish the enemies, and bring in His own long predicted and glorious reign of everlasting blessedness upon the earth.

9

The Fatal Omission

To some extent it has been necessary to anticipate the subject of this chapter in dealing with those counterfeits which are predicted for the last days, when there will be found a "form of godliness, denying the power thereof," and also the deep "doctrines of devils" which are "lies in hypocrisy." This chapter deals with that which is vital in the true faith, and which is to be so carefully omitted in the false faith—that which makes the true so potent, and without which the false becomes an immeasurable deception. Everything depends upon this one point of distinction; for, according to prophecy, it is the only difference that is finally to exist between the false and the true. The issue is, therefore, as important as life itself.

It has already been seen that the method of counterfeiting, if successful, will require Satan to appropriate and incorporate in his false systems every available principle of the true, for the deception of the counterfeit depends wholly upon its likeness to the real. By this is revealed the reason for calling that a lie or deception which is externally so like the truth. Certainly there could be no greater pitfall for souls than a system which seems to be the truth of God, and yet robs its followers of any basis for a true hope, and it will be found that the strongest condemnation of the Bible is uttered against such systems and their promoters.

In seeking to discover the actual point of difference between the false and the true, it will be well, first, to consider the present perverted relation which exists between the Creator and the fallen human creature; for herein is revealed the necessity for that which God proposes to accomplish by redemption.

Two important points in Satan's doctrine were announced by him in the Garden of Eden when he first approached the woman, and these two declarations have been an important part of the world's creeds throughout the history of man. The first was a bold denial of a positive statement of God, when Satan said: "Ye shall not surely die." Whether Satan intended here simply to deny the truth of God's statement, or whether he overestimated his own resources and proposed to shield them from their God-appointed doom, is not clear. Certainly the latter view is in keeping with Satan's original purpose, as well as with his evident sincerity. It is quite reasonable to conclude that, if he could be so misguided as to attempt to be like the Most High, he would willingly have undertaken to protect man from judgment which followed as a result of loyalty to himself. Satan is striving, at any rate, to direct the lives of those who are under his power into a degree of self development that will be a substitute for the revealed purpose of God for men.

The second announcement of Satan assured the woman that they would, by this independent action, "be as gods"; and this, so far from promising death, seemed to them the immediate realization of the highest ideal. The consummation of this ideal is thus described: "For whom he did foreknow, he also did predestinate to be conformed to the image of his Son" (Rom. 8:29). "Beloved, now are we the sons of God, and it doth not yet appear what we shall be: but we know that, when he shall appear, we shall be like him; for we shall see him as he is" (1 John 3:2). "When Christ, who is our life, shall appear, then shall ye also appear with him in glory" (Col. 3:4). "Now unto him that is able to keep you from falling, and to present you faultless before the presence of his glory with exceeding joy" (Jude 24). "For our citizenship is in heaven; whence also we wait for a Savior, the Lord Jesus Christ: who shall fashion anew the body of our humiliation, that it may be conformed to the body of his glory, according to the working whereby he is able even to subject all things unto himself" (Phil. 3:20, 21, R.V.).

It is natural that Satan should suggest to humanity that which had been the objective of his own unholy ambition; and especially is it natural, since by such a separation of humanity from its God, he could claim that authority over them, and secure that worship from them which he so much craved.

There are, then, at least two distinct methods proposed for the uplifting of humanity, and these are brought into sharp contrast; for one is of Satan, and the other is of God. Since both these methods claim to aim at the same end—though one ideal is not worthy to be compared with the other— the method, alone, forms the first point for discussion.

Under the Satanic control man has always been strangely influenced in the matter of his relation to his Creator. He, too, has been willing to assume a hopeless position of independence toward God; and, under that abnormal relation, he has gone out alone to grope his way, blindly seeking to build his own character, and by education and cultivation to improve his natural heart which God has pronounced humanly incurable. He has also bent his inventive skill to the development of means by which God-imposed labor may be avoided, and much of his selfish greed springs from a desire to purchase a substitute who shall bear for him the discomfort of a sweating brow. "God is not in all his thoughts"; nor has he any disposition to claim the help of God under the terms upon which it is offered. The Satanic method for life prompts him to attempt to become a god by a process of self-help and development of the finite resources.

It is possible to introduce much of religious form into the world system of self-help; for there is a great field for religious exercise for the one who is attempting to make himself God-like, and there is endless material for supplication and prayer that all available assistance may be secured to aid one in that humanly impossible task. A devout spirit is, therefore, a part of the Satanic doctrine, and the predicted "forms of godliness" will naturally appear.

There is a vast difference between an individual supplicating God to save him: and one supplicating God to help him save himself. The latter is a part of the Satanic plan and has no promise of divine favor upon it. All such religious exercise, though full of outward forms and deep sincerity, leaves its moral aspirants doomed, alike with the most degraded, to an everlasting separation and banishment from the presence of God. Prayer and religious practice do not really place the saving work in the hands of God, but mockingly ask Him to give His sanction and assistance to that which wholly dishonors and disregards Him, and which is also both unreasonable and impossible.

Though the process by which unfallen man would have reached a higher development has not been revealed, it is certain that he would have been then, as now, wholly dependent upon the Creator. Man's present independence toward God is the blindest delusion of the fallen nature, for complete independence cannot even be assumed in the least of all temporal things. How much less is it possible to be independent in that which is spiritual!

Again, the self-saving principle is utter folly, since God must demand a quality which no human being can present. God's requirement is not unreasonable, however, for He also proposes to bestow, in grace, all that He ever demands. The absolute righteousness of God demands no less than absolute righteousness in all who are acceptable to Him; yet He has never mocked man by asking him to make himself acceptable, or even to attempt to do it by divine help. True salvation is wholly a work of God, and provides a standing in Christ which is the very righteousness of God. It is said to be both a finished work and a gift, and, therefore, it lays no obligation upon the saved one to complete it himself, or to make after payments of service for it; though the saved one is called upon to serve from another and more glorious motive.

The divine terms of obtainment into Godlikeness are clearly stated in the scriptures. However, the estimate God has placed upon human nature at its best, and the logical necessity that man shall receive, as a gift, all that he has, and be forever a debtor to the divine giver, have always been rejected by self-sufficient and Satan-inspired humanity. These terms are the only possible or reasonable relations that could rightfully exist between fallen humanity and its Creator. At this point Satan has blinded the minds of the lost lest they should believe, and he has made that which is reasonable and natural seem to be unreasonable and unnatural. The unsaved are unable to abandon their Satan-inspired sense of self-sufficiency and independence of God and receive from Him, as a gift, every quality which is commendable in His sight.

The controversy between Satan-ruled man and God is one of method. It is one of self-righteousness and character building, or one of bestowed righteousness and character by the fruit of the Spirit. Will man try to save himself, or humbly submit to being saved by Another? Will he try to conform himself to what little he knows to be good and true, or will he be transformed by the power of God into that which is no less than the image of Christ? Will he present the sacrifice of a sincere effort to be moral and religious or accept the God-provided sacrifice for all sin in the shed blood of Christ? Will he try to establish himself before God on the ground of his own works, or rest in the finished work of Christ for him? Will he try to improve his fallen nature, or partake of the divine nature and become a son of God by the power of God, through faith in Christ Jesus!

One method, it may be seen, depends wholly upon self for its realization, promises glory to man alone, and has its origin at that unknown time when Satan proposed in his heart to become like the Most High. The other method is dependent upon God alone, and, therefore, demands an attitude of faith toward Him for its realization, and issues in glory to the Creator, who alone is worthy to be praised. The latter, in contrast with Satan's method, had its origin in the purpose of God, which He purposed before the foundation of the world. Therein, transcendent blessings are offered, stores of grace are unfolded, and the omnipotent power of God is seen working for the transformation of His human creatures. These two methods are confused only because they seem to aim at the same general result. In reality their results, like their methods, are not only incomparable, but they are as far removed from each other as God's ways are higher than man's ways.

The revelation from God in regard to salvation might have been limited to the fact that He, rather than man, was to accomplish the work; and while much that is involved in the mighty undertaking of redemption has not been, and probably cannot be, reduced to the level of human understanding, He saw fit to reveal much that was necessary, on both the God-ward and the man-ward side, in providing this way of salvation. No human conception of the atonement is complete. Notwithstanding this, the all-sufficient sacrificial death of Christ being clearly stated in the scriptures, its value, though unanalyzed, may be appropriated; for man is not saved by what he comprehends or understands, but his salvation is made possible by his attitude of willingness and expectation toward the saving power of Christ.

In determining the exact point of the truth that is to be omitted from the Satanic counterfeit, it is important to distinguish between the *Person* and *work* of Christ. In the one is included His teachings and example, both in His life and death; in the other is included His substitutionary, sacrificial, and atoning death for the sin of the world. There is no controversy as to the value of the teachings and example of Jesus, but the wisdom of this world is displayed in ever-increasing antagonism against the blood of the cross. This enmity has never been founded on the Word of God, for scripture does not deny itself. The opposition appeals to pride and human reason, and dares to challenge the plain statements of the Bible on this particular point. Very much is thus omitted; for all the meaning of sacrifice in the Old Testament and all the promises of redemption in the New Testament are inseparably related to the blood of the cross. It may be to the Jew a stumbling block, and to the Greek foolishness; yet to those who are called, both Jews and Greeks, "it is the power of God and the wisdom of God."

In Ephesians, the eternal purpose of God is said to be the complete perfection of believers: "According as he hath chosen us in him before the foundation of the world, that we should be holy and without blame before him in love" (1:4). And that transformation is also said to be by the blood of Christ: "In whom we have redemption through his blood, the forgiveness of sins, according to the riches of his grace" (1:7). In like manner the object of this transformation is said to be that the church may be the present and eternal manifestation of the wisdom, love and power of God: "To the intent that now unto the principalities and powers in heavenly places might be known by the church the manifold wisdom of God" (3:10). "That in the ages to come he might show the exceeding riches of his grace in his kindness toward us through Christ Jesus" (2:7). "And what is the exceeding greatness of his power to usward who believe, according to the working of his mighty power, which he wrought in Christ, when he raised him from the dead, and set him at his own right hand in the heavenly places" (1:19, 20).

There is also a strong contrast of figures used in the Old Testament which accurately emphasizes the mighty power of the Creator in the regeneration of a soul. In Psalm 8:3 the creation of the solar system is mentioned as the work of the *fingers* of God: "When I consider thy heavens, the work of thy *fingers*, the moon and the stars, which thou hast ordained," but in Isa. 53:1, where the substitutionary sacrifice of Christ is referred to, it is spoken of as the effort of the Creator's *arm*: "Who hath believed our report? and to whom is the arm of the Lord revealed?" The suggestion here given, that the creation of a universe is the work of His fingers, and the regeneration of souls is the work of His mighty arm, is not overdrawn; for the price of redemption cannot be measured by corruptible things, such as gold and silver: but is purchased at the price of the precious blood of Christ, as of a lamb without blemish and without spot (1 Pet. 1:19).

The Scriptures abound in statements that regeneration, and the whole transforming work of redemption, are accomplished on the ground of the sacrificial blood of the cross; and if these statements of the Bible are rejected, the discussion can never be one of interpretation of the Scriptures, but becomes a question of the authority of the testimony of the Bible. A few of these passages are here given: "Surely he hath borne our griefs, and carried our sorrows: yet we did esteem him stricken, smitten of God, and afflicted. But he was wounded for our transgressions, he was bruised for our iniquities: the chastisement of our peace was upon him; and with his stripes we are healed. All we like sheep have gone astray; we have turned every one to his own way; and the Lord hath laid on him the iniquity of us all" (Isa. 53:4-6). "Even as the Son of man came not to be ministered unto, but to minister, and to give his life a ransom for many" (Matt. 20:28). "Behold the Lamb of God, which taketh away the sin of the world" (John 1:29). "Whom God hath set forth to be a propitiation through faith in his blood" (Rom. 3:25). "But God commendeth his love toward us, in that, while we were yet sinners, Christ died for us. Much more then, being now justified by his blood, we shall be saved from wrath through him" (Rom. 5:8, 9): "For he hath made him to be sin for us, who knew no sin; that we might be made the righteousness of God in him" (2 Cor. 5:21). "Who gave himself for our sins, that he might deliver us from this present evil world, according to the will of God and our Father" (Gal. 1:4). "And every priest standeth daily ministering and offering oftentimes the same sacrifices, which can never take away sins: but this man, after he had offered one sacrifice for sins forever, sat down on the right hand of God; from henceforth expecting till his enemies be made his footstool. For by one offering he hath perfected forever them that are sanctified" (Heb. 10:11-14). "Who his own self bare our sins in his own body on the tree, that we, being dead to sins, should live unto righteousness: by whose stripes ye were healed" (1 Pet. 2:24). "For Christ also hath once suffered for sins, the just for the unjust, that he might bring us to God, being put to death in the flesh, but quickened by the Spirit" (1 Pet. 3:18). "And he is the propitiation for our sins: and not for ours only, but also for the sins of the whole world" (1 John 2:2).

From the foregoing passages it may be seen that, according to the Scriptures, the stupendous transformation of regeneration is not only the greatest divine undertaking, but is directly accomplished on the grounds of the sacrificial death and shed blood of Christ, and is sealed in security by the Holy Spirit of promise.

The sacrificial death of Christ presents the only gateway for fallen man from the power and final doom of Satan to the glory and transcendent light of God; and there is nothing strange in the Satan-inspired "offence of the cross" which is often garnished with culture, worldly wisdom, and religious forms. Even in Paul's time there were those who were enemies of the cross of Christ: "For many walk, of whom I have told you often, and now tell you even weeping, that they are the enemies of the cross of Christ" (Phil. 3:18). There were evidently recognized leaders in the Christian fellowship, who were undoubtedly ardent admirers of the *Person* of Jesus, as revealed in His earthly life and example; yet Paul does not hesitate to mention his own tears at the fatal omission in their preaching, for they were enemies of the cross of Christ.

Again, it is predicted in 2 Peter 2:1, 2 that a fierce enmity against the cross should appear: "But there were false prophets also among the people, even as there shall be false teachers among you, who privily shall bring in damnable heresies, even denying the Lord that bought them, and bring upon themselves swift destruction. And many shall follow their pernicious ways; by reason of whom the way of truth shall be evil spoken of." Here again the denial is against the purchase or redeeming *work* of Christ rather than His Person or character. They are offended at the Lord who *bought* them, though they may be devoted to the Lord who *taught* them. These Satanic agents are described here, as before, as those who seem to be teachers in the true faith, yet they bring in damnable heresies, in all covered subtlety, crystallizing in a denial of the redemption that is in Christ. Being only blinded unregenerate men, they may suppose themselves to be ministers of righteousness and apostles of Christ. Their humanitarian dreams may inspire tireless effort and zeal, their doctrine may become world-wide in its influence, and they may drive their mighty ecclesiastical machinery by the injunctions of scripture; yet if the curtain could be lifted, their "angel of light" would be found to be Satan, working through them to resist the purpose of God, and themselves the ministers of Satan, speaking lies in hypocrisy, having their conscience seared as with a hot iron, daring in their exalted position to devitalize the Gospel of its power unto salvation, and dragging immortal souls after them into hell.

It is not strange that there is resentment against the mystery of the cross which does not exist against any other inexplicable fact in the world. It is not strange that the ministers of Satan, appearing as the apostles of Christ and ministers of righteousness, should fortify their lies and hypocrisies by contending for almost every phase of revealed truth, grounding their authority so positively in the scriptures of Truth; yet subtly omitting, or violently denying, the one and only point upon which the interests of God and Satan divide. It is not strange that there is a wide call for a "restatement of the truth," which usually proposes to omit the new birth and substitute self-effort to be good and character building in its place. It is not strange that the wise and cultured of this world feel their aesthetic natures shocked by the doctrine of redemption by blood, yet entertain no sense of their own abhorrent pollution in the sight of the infinitely holy One. It is not strange that the world assumes to have advanced beyond that which is repeatedly said to be the manifestation of the wisdom of God; branding as bigots, insincere, or ignorant, all who still hold to the whole testimony of God. It is not strange that the atonement by blood is omitted, for it is Satan's hour and the power of darkness. The child of God must bear the ever-increasing reproaches of his crucified Lord, until the glory dawns and the shadows flee away.

10

Modern Devices

It has been the privilege and duty of the church throughout her history to be looking for the return of the One to whom she has been espoused. Had her eyes never wandered from that expectant gaze, she would have been saved much sorrow and shame at His coming, for she has lost her scriptural character and much of her witnessing power whenever she has said, "My Lord delayeth his coming." It is then that she has fallen to beating the manservants and the maidservants, and has become drunken with the wine of this world.

True devotion to Christ must naturally issue in a deep desire to be with Him and to see Him face to face, and though it is quite possible to have been misled or untaught in regard to the conditions of His coming, the contemplation of such a promise from Him can but kindle a glowing hope in a truly devoted heart. It is a direct contradiction to claim supreme affection for Him, and yet be careless of His promised return, or wholly contented while separated from Him. The world, that cannot comprehend such devotion to Christ, will easily chide the believer, and denounce him for what they now call his "other worldness" when his affections are set on things above "where Christ sitteth at the right hand of God," and when his heart rejoices in the certain hope that "when Christ, who is our life, shall appear, then shall ye also appear with him in glory."

It was necessary for Satan to rob the church, to a great extent, of her "blessed hope" of Christ's return, before he could attract attention to his own attempts at world improvement, and establish his own authority as ruler over this age. Expectation along the God-appointed lines must be abandoned, for the most part, before humanity can be federated, and religious institutions be made to cooperate in the Satanic program.

This vital key-truth of the imminent return of Christ was, therefore, first discredited, and then followed by an attack upon the deity of the Son of God and His sacrificial death; which attack is ever increasing, and must increase to the very end. The body of truth concerning the Lord's return is so extensive that there have always been some humble and devout souls who have dared to believe His promises, and thus the real Church, to some extent, her watch has been keeping.

The mighty tool in Satan's hands for the destroying of the hope of Christ's coming has been a simple one: zealous souls have been found who, ignoring the statements of the scriptures, would attempt to fix the day of His coming. Then, as their prophecy failed of fulfillment, the world and many in the church have laughed them to scorn. Unfortunately they came to laugh also at the very promise of God, saying, "Where is the promise of his coming?" and in so doing they have fulfilled some of the very things that are predicted for the end of the age: "Knowing this first, that there shall come in the last days scoffers, walking after their own lusts [desires], and saying, Where is the promise of his coming for since the fathers fell asleep, all things continue as they were from the beginning of the creation" (2 Pet. 3:3, 4). Thus Satan's authority is being established.

The exact time of Christ's return has not been revealed, nor will it be announced by a prophet. Nevertheless, the "children of light and the children of the day" "are not in darkness that day should overtake them as a thief" (1 Thess. 5:4, 5). It is their privilege to rejoice in every promise of His coming, and to recognize every new indication of His nearness as eagerly as the betrothed awaits her beloved. The true believer's glory, as well as his union with loved ones in Christ, is imminent, and by faith he can look beyond the days of the earth's greatest anguish and, seeing the triumph of all blessedness, rejoice in the hope of his Lord's coming, and pray, "Even so, come, Lord Jesus."

It is, therefore, impossible to know how much of time yet

remains for the gathering out of the Bride and the development of Satan's rule; yet it is evident that within the last generation the exact fulfillment of those things which are predicted for the last days has begun, and is even now developing faster than the mind can comprehend.

Not all the signs of the times have a place in these pages, but only such as are directly connected with the working of Satan.

Since the blood redemption of the cross is the central truth and value of the true faith, it being the "power of God unto salvation" (Rom. 1:16; 1 Cor. 1:23, 24), any counterfeit system of doctrine which would omit this essential, must force some secondary truth into the place of prominence. Any of the great scriptural subjects which are of universal interest to humanity, such as physical health, life after death, morality, unfulfilled prophecy, or religious forms, may be substituted in the false systems for that which is vital. And while those subjects are all found in their proper relations and importance in the true faith, the fact that people are universally inclined to give attention to them furnishes an opportunity for Satan to make a strong appeal to humanity through them, using these subjects as central truths in his false and counterfeit systems. Many are easily led to fix their attention upon the secondary things, and to neglect wholly the one primary thing. Especially is this true since the secondary things are tangible and seen; while the one essential thing is spiritual and unseen, and Satan has blinded their eyes toward that which is of eternal value.

A system of doctrine may, then, be formed which includes every truth of the scriptures save one— exalting the *Person* of Christ, but not His atoning *work*, and emphasizing some secondary truth as its central value. This system will be readily accepted by blinded humanity, though the real power of God unto salvation has been carefully withdrawn.

Naturally it would be supposed that such Satan-inspired systems would have no value or power, since there could be no divine favor upon them. Such a supposition would be possible only because of the prevailing misunderstanding as to the real power of Satan. If the description given of him in the scriptures is accepted, he will be seen to be possessed with miraculous power— able to perform such marvels that the whole world is led to wonder and then to worship. He is free also to bestow this miraculous power upon others (Rev. 13:2). So it is no marvel if his ministers, who appear as the ministers of righteousness, are able to exert superhuman power when it is directly in the interest of the Satanic projects.

The great power of Satan has doubtless been active along these lines during all the ages past; for it is impossible that humanity should have worshipped other gods blindly without some recompense, and it is Satan himself who has been thus worshipped (Lev. 17:7; 2 Chron. 11:15; Rev. 9:20).

It is not final evidence, therefore, that a system of doctrine is of God simply because there are accompanying manifestations of superhuman power; nor is it final evidence that the Almighty has responded, simply because any form of supplication has been answered. The divine movements are, of necessity, limited by the laws of His own holiness, and access into His presence is by the blood of Jesus alone, by a new and living Way which was consecrated for us through His flesh (Heb. 10:19, 20). Assuming to come before God in prayer, but ignoring this truth, is but to insult with pollution, Him who is infinitely holy and pure. Satan, who is aspiring to the place of the Almighty, may answer the prayer of his own subjects even though that prayer is blindly addressed to the Supreme Being. Surely the Satan-ruled world does not come before God by the blood of Jesus.

Though false systems of doctrine have always existed, counterfeits in hypocrisy are a distinct characteristic of the last days of the present age. And it is a most significant fact that within the last generation such systems have appeared and are rapidly multiplying—systems that borrow every phase of the true faith, but one, and are conspicuous in that they emphasize some secondary truth with what seems, at times, to be miraculous power. Multitudes are being won to these creeds, both because of their apparent religious aspect, and by the actual results which they accomplish.

There is probably no subject of more universal interest than that of physical health; and but recently "Christian Science," which chiefly emphasizes physical health, has appeared. While it gathers into itself some elements that are foreign both to Christianity and to science, and appropriates much from the field of psychology, it assumes to be an infallible interpretation of the scriptures, and makes Jesus its highest exponent and teacher. Yet it positively denies even the reality of sin and the need of Christ's atoning sacrifice. Its followers are won and held by its religious claims, and by the actual physical and mental transformations that are secured. Nothing but ignorance will attempt to deny that, to some extent, its claims are real. That it has assemblies, ministers, and mysteries deep and profound, and that it is able to demonstrate its claims of physical transformation, does not lift it above the level of Satan's power. That it denies even the need of the blood of the cross, separates it, in spite of its claims, from the God of the scriptures, and brands it with every characteristic of Satan's counterfeit.

Another subject, already mentioned, which is of common interest to humanity, is that of life after death. How persistently man has sought to see beyond the veil! And yet how little of fact has been discovered, beyond that which it has pleased God to reveal in His Word! How strong is the desire of the heart to follow the departed into the great unseen! And how subtle is "Spiritism" in its election of the question of a future state as its bait to beguile sorrow-crushed souls into a disregard of their only hope in the blood of Christ!

This system has existed from the earliest ages and has the unqualified condemnation of the Bible; yet in the last half-century it has taken new interest and dignity to itself under the modern title of "Psychical Research." With boldest assumption it claims to be the only safe exponent of truth, and to be working in the interests of science— changing science being accepted as more trustworthy than revelation.

Less is made of the Scriptures in this system than in Christian Science. Yet here, as might be expected, there is violent opposition to the doctrine of redemption from sin.

"Spiritism" bases its claims on the supposed testimony of departed spirits and it cannot be denied but that there is an intelligent response to the human appeal from the unseen, and messages are being received and mysterious acts are being performed with increasing frequency. It cannot be proven, however, that this response is from the spirit of the person named, for a lying spirit could easily know enough of any person's life to represent him in every detail. That the whole system could be of Satan is evident, and since it denies man's only hope of redemption, it is no part of the real truth of God. It, too, bears all the marks of the workings of Satan.

Another system of thought called "New," but which is as old as human philosophy, appropriates every phase of metaphysical belief. The central idea of "New Thought" is the complete development of man—body, soul, and spirit. Every possible human power is utilized; there is recognition of the Creator; the Word of God is appropriated in convenient texts; and Christ is claimed by its followers to be the complete example and embodiment of all their ideals. Newly stated theories of psychology are included in this system, and the whole teaching stands as the embodiment of all the ideals of the one who first suggested to humanity that they, by their own efforts, become as gods. The system wholly denies scriptural regeneration, both as to its necessity and as a fact; and is a veritable worship of self, as predicted for the last days (2 Tim. 3:2). It substitutes the development of the will as a power for victory in the life, in place of the God-provided victory over sin by the Spirit. Its followers seem to be utterly blind to the plainest truths of the scriptures, and are marvelling at what they suppose to be a discovery, when, perchance, they are able to comprehend some secondary truth of the Word of God. This system, like "Christian Science," numbers its followers by the hundreds of thousands. They support many periodicals, and their teachings are read and accepted throughout the world.

There is also another system known as "Millennial Dawnism,"[1] and by other organization names, which relies upon its interpretation of prophecy to secure the interest of its followers. There is universal interest in the future, and by means of Millennial Dawnism, Satan is covering the most erroneous teachings concerning salvation and the Person and work of Christ through an emphasis upon the prophetic scriptures which satisfies the natural craving for knowledge concerning "things to come."

In all these doctrines there is included much of the precious

---

1. The sect known today as Jehovah's Witnesses.

truth of God, but this is employed only as a bait to cover the relentless hook of Satan, by which he seeks to draw human souls away from God and into perdition. Not one positive word is said of the future state of man, or of his fitness to meet his God, and any belief in immortality is borrowed from the revelation of God; for the systems themselves are given over to distracting and diverting man from the thought of his need of a divinely wrought preparation for eternity. It is commonly stated by the followers of these systems that it is of little importance what one believes, for it is the *life* that counts. Thus the great and necessary fact that any true character as well as salvation depends upon what one believes, rather than on the life, is discredited.

These systems are mentioned only as examples of the almost innumerable doctrines that are sweeping the world today. They often reappear under new and misleading titles. The truth they acknowledge, and many forces they employ, are, in their right relationships, God's gracious provision for His saints; yet when these truths and forces are used alone, where the real purpose of God is skillfully omitted, they become only the hypocrisy that covers and garnishes a lie.

Again, many are deluded by the emphasis upon the mere outward forms of the visible church. When these forms are analyzed, they appear to represent a church ministered to by a recognized ordained minister who depends upon his own personality for his power; and who preaches ethics and morality drawn from scripture texts and other ethical writings. Prayers are offered, imploring the Almighty to aid humanity in its attempts to commend itself to Him by a more or less faithful practice of religion. The pleasures of music as an art are provided at extravagant cost, in place of the praise that is inspired by the Spirit of God. Social gatherings are held, to take the place of the unity of the Spirit and the love of the brethren. Humanitarian appeals for the betterment of the world are made, in place of the evangelical regeneration by the cross; and not one reference to the real Gospel is made from one year to the next, unless it be in a covered denial. The sleeping congregations are seemingly satisfied with a mockery of the truth, and are content with a doctrine which proposes to educate souls into hell, and which encourages them to make a few efforts toward self-development while on their certain road to perdition. It is no longer good form in society to be without some church relationships, yet the one and only true basis for salvation may never have been comprehended or accepted by a multitude of these members. Truly the god of this world is accomplishing his end, and his blinded followers are coming to be numbered with the faithful. The evil birds are flocking to the mustard tree, and the corrupting leaven is permeating the measures of meal.

The last development of the earth history of the visible church is predicted to be a condition in which she is saying, "I am rich, and increased with goods, and have need of nothing." The passage continues, "and knowest not that thou art wretched, and miserable, and poor, and blind, and naked. I counsel thee to buy of me gold tried in the fire, that thou mayest be rich; and white raiment, that thou mayest be clothed, and that the shame of thy nakedness do not appear; and anoint thine eyes with eyesalve, that thou mayest see. As many as I love, I rebuke and chasten: be zealous therefore, and repent. Behold, I stand at the door and knock: if any man hear my voice, and open the door, I will come in to him, and will sup with him, and he with me" (Rev. 3:17-20). If scripture language and figure mean anything, this is a description of an unregenerate church over which the Lord is pleading. It is from this church that He has withdrawn, and is seen outside, standing and knocking. His hope is not centered upon reforming the whole mass of professing members, for His offer is to the individual, "any man," with whom He will then have personal communion and fellowship.

Sad is the spectacle of these churches, meeting week after week to be beguiled by the philosophy of men, and raising no voice in protest against the denial of their only foundation as a church, and of their only hope for time and eternity! Far more honorable were the infidels of the past generation than these ministers. They were wholly outside the church. But now, behold the inconsistency! Men who are covered by the vesture of the church, ministering its sacraments, and supported by its benevolence, are making an open attack upon that wisdom of God which made Christ Jesus the only ground for all righteousness, sanctification, and redemption. The predictions for the last days are thus not only being fulfilled by false systems and doctrines, but they are found in the visible church itself. "For the time will come when they will not endure sound doctrine; but after their own lusts shall they heap to themselves teachers, having itching ears; and they shall turn away their ears from the truth, and shall be turned unto fables" (2 Tim. 4:3, 4).

Great religious activities are possible without coming into complications with saving faith. It is possible to be more concerned over the untimely death of one hundred thousand drunkards than with the Christless death of twenty million human beings, or to be wholly concerned with the educational and physical needs of the heathen and to neglect their greatest need in regeneration. Thus Satan may gain his own ends, even through some so-called missionary undertakings, for in this manner he can beguile untaught saints to limit their work to the lines of his highest ideals. It is possible to fight against sin and not present the Savior, or to urge the highest scriptural ideals and yet offer no reasonable way of attainment.

There is a strange fascination about these undertakings which are humanitarian, and are religious only in form and title. And there is a strange attractiveness in the leader who announces that he is not concerned with the doctrines of the Bible, because the helping of humanity is his one passion and care: yet his passion is lost and his care is to no real end unless coupled with a very positive message of a particular way of salvation, the true understanding of which demands a series of most careful distinctions.

Recently the word "pragmatism" has been brought into popular use to denote the test by which the pragmatists measure all systems, theories and doctrines. The pragmatic inquiry when applied to any system, theory, or doctrine may be understood to mean, "does it meet its claims in practice?" Although much is being made of this phase of pragmatism, the test is as old as the race, and is verified by the Bible, for Jesus said, "By their fruits ye shall know them." However, the burden of testing claims has never before been so great, for the world was never so filled with new and strange theories as now. And these modern systems that deny true salvation in Christ are growing mightily under this test. They offer comparatively little and are usually able to meet their claims. "Christian Science" does, to some extent, change the condition of mind and body. "Spiritism" offers demonstrations from the invisible, and the demonstrations appear. "New Thought" proposes a development of the whole natural man, and thrives by the practical test of "pragmatism." The same is true of all other similar systems and doctrines, and will be true of those that may yet appear, since it is the very program of Satan as it is revealed in his last blasphemous counterfeit of the Son of God; for it is written in Revelation 13:3, 4 that they first wondered at the miracles of the "Beast," and then worshiped. Woe to the untaught soul who stands wondering today at the marvels of this evil age, if he be without a sense of the importance and value of the priceless blood of the cross! The step is not far for such an one to the place where he falls in worship—worship of a being who is supposed to have forgotten abhorrence of sin and abandoned all eternal covenants of mercy by blood alone; a being who is supposed to be glad that the world has outgrown the old unbearable estimates of sin and redemption, the abiding difference between the saved and the unsaved, and into whose presence the worshiper is supposed to be free to come on the ground of his fallen human nature, and on the ground of the "universal fatherhood of God and the universal brotherhood of man."

The new situation consists in the attempt of the enemy to keep the outward form of our faith, quoting scripture and eulogizing Christ, but denying every word of saving grace. This gigantic monster of confusion began in Germany and has been largely accepted over the civilized earth. Germany's military conquest is small compared with her spiritual conquest. Her armies may be defeated, but her unbelief is cursing the world. These "doctrines of devils" which devitalize truth by denying redemption through the blood of Christ were all predicted and were to be God's sign to us of the presence of the "last days." What more evidence do we need that these days are already here?

Who can be the god of these systems? the energizing power in these people? and the answerer of their prayers? Surely not the God of the Scriptures who cannot deny Himself, and whose word cannot be made to pass away! Revelation sets forth but one other being who is capable of these undertakings; and it not only assigns to this being a great and sufficient motive for all such activity, but clearly predicts that he will thus "oppose" and "exalt himself" in this very day and age.

Much of the secondary truth is the present inheritance of the child of God. However, if there is a choice to be made the deepest wisdom will perceive that all the combined secondary values which Satan can offer are but for a fleeting time, and are not worthy to be compared with the eternal riches of grace in Christ Jesus.

11

The Believer's Present Position

Since the Bible contains God's message to the people of all ages, it must be rightly divided if the body of truth concerning any particular age or people is to be clearly understood. There are, undoubtedly, many things in common in the various ages, and because of that fact the superficial use of the scriptures has been to treat the entire Book as a direct message to all people of all time. This method, as has been stated, has resulted in great confusion concerning the divine program.

When that portion of the Bible which directly applies to the present age has been discovered, that, too, must be divided; for the present time is a period of mixture among the people of the earth—the saints of God tenting among the citizens of the Satanic system, and having nothing in common with them beyond the ordinary things of this earth life.

Again, that particular body of truth which applies to the child of God in this age may be divided, and a portion be called "positional truth" because it unfolds the believer's present relation to the Godhead, the heavenlies, and the present world: while another portion may be known as "life truth" because it specifically sets forth the believer's present responsibility in conduct and service, and also includes the provisions of God whereby the saved one may fully accomplish the whole will of God. A partial study of life truth is reserved for the next and last chapter, while this chapter is to be devoted to the believer's present position and separation from the world.

The importance of positional truth is suggested by the fact

that in several contexts of the scriptures where it is treated, it precedes the statement of life truth, forming the basis of its appeal. As an illustration of this it may be seen that the order of the doctrinal Epistles is first, to state a great positional truth which is then followed by an appeal for a life consistent with the truth revealed.

The first section of the book of Romans (chapters 1–8) sets forth the fact of salvation which is the work of God alone. This is followed (omitting the dispensational parenthesis of chapters 9–11) by the closing section (chapters 12–16), which is a detailed description of the life a saved person should live, and opens with this appeal: "I beseech you therefore, brethren, by the mercies of God, that ye present your bodies a living sacrifice, holy, acceptable unto God, which is your reasonable service. And be not conformed to this world: but be ye transformed by the renewing of your mind, that ye may prove what is that good, and acceptable, and perfect, will of God." So, in the first section of the letter to the Ephesians (chapters 4–6), the believer's position is unfolded, and this is followed by a section (chapters 4–6), which is a series of injunctions for a heavenly walk. This section opens as follows: "I therefore, the prisoner of the Lord, beseech you that ye walk worthy of the vocation wherewith ye are called, with all lowliness and meekness, with longsuffering, forbearing one another in love; endeavoring to keep the unity of the Spirit in the bond of peace." No appeal for faithfulness in the Christian life will be found to be adequate or effective that does not follow this same order, or that is not based upon some revealed fact of the new life in Christ. It is probable that the present neglect and disregard of positional truth has, in spite of moral exhortation, borne its legitimate fruit in a time-serving worldly church.

It is a beautiful example of the harmony of the scriptures that, while the evil of the present age is so clearly described, the true child of God is most carefully separated from its relationships, and is seen to be in a position so independent of all the authority of the world that he may walk with the Lord in unbroken communion and fellowship, even while surrounded by this spiritual darkness. And, though the scriptural statements as to the ever increasing darkness of this age be rejected, no meaning can be given to these passages which separate the believer from this world without the recognition of the black background of the failure and sinfulness of this age. It is noticeable that the modern systems take no notice of the difference between the saved and the unsaved, as they also make little of the future state. This is in accordance with the fact that both of these truths are wholly dependent upon regeneration; and that is the one truth which false systems were originated by Satan to resist.

The Bible presents the widest distinction between the saved and the unsaved. The distinction is fundamental. The Bible teaches that the unsaved are dead in trespasses and sins, while the saved possess a new divine life (Eph. 2:1, 2) the unsaved are energized by Satan (Eph. 2:2), while the saved are energized by God (Phil. 2:13) the unsaved are in the power of darkness, while the saved are translated into the kingdom of God's dear Son (Col. 1:13) the unsaved are asleep in the arms of the wicked one (1 John 5:19), while the saved are safe in the hand of God (John 10:29) and hid in Christ (Col. 3:3). It is significant that this important body of truth never appears in any one of the Satanic counterfeit systems of faith today.

The Christian has been placed in at least thirty-three positions in his relation to God in salvation, seven of which are considered here. Three to be named concern his change from the darkness of Satan to the light of God; two concern his relationship to the heavenly sphere; and two concern his relationship to the Satanic order. A careful study of all the passages in which the positions are unfolded will reveal the great reality of redemption.[1]

The first divine movement toward the salvation of an individual, after the prayer of intercession through the Spirit, is illumination by the Spirit. This same work is also mentioned as the "convicting" or "convincing" of the Spirit. In this part of the divine undertaking the blinding by Satan is removed and the soul beholds, by divine vision, the Lord of glory and the way into eternal life through Him.

---

1. A complete treatment of all the believer's positions resulting from the work of God in redemption will be found in the author's book, *Salvation*.

This illuminating work of the Spirit is mentioned by Paul in his words to King Agrippa, wherein he describes his own commission to service. He claimed to have been appointed by the Lord who spoke to him from the Glory. He relates that by this commission he was sent "to open their eyes, and to turn them from darkness to light, and from the power of Satan unto God, that they may receive forgiveness of sins, and inheritance among them which are sanctified by faith that is in me" (Acts 26:18). This is the exact order of the divine movements in redemption. The illumination of the Spirit is placed before everything else. There is probably no more neglected truth in modern evangelism than this preliminary work of the Spirit: yet it is the divine preparation for the intelligent action of the human will, and if the right choice is made it unveils the eyes for time and eternity.

This important illuminating work of the Spirit is more fully described in John 16:8-11 as being a revelation of the judgment, by the cross, of all sin and condemnation; the vision of the glorious righteous Christ, now in heaven; and the realization of the sin of rejecting Him. The passage is here given: "Nevertheless I tell you the truth; it is expedient for you that I go away: for if I go not away, the Comforter will not come unto you; but if I depart, I will send him unto you. And when he is come, he will reprove [convince] the world of sin, and of righteousness, and of judgment: of sin, because they believe not on me; of righteousness, because I go to my Father, and ye see me no more; of judgment, because the prince of this world is judged." The true child of God is, then, one in whom the Spirit has wrought in lifting the blinding by Satan and revealing to some extent, even now, the surpassing glory of Christ. Sin, too, has become a reality, and the cross and the precious blood have become the basis of his confidence toward his God.

Another revelation concerning the present position of the believer is that he has partaken of the divine nature through regeneration by the Spirit. This truth is stated in many passages, a few of which are here given: "But as many as received him, to them gave he power to become the sons of God, even to them that believe on his name: which were born, not of blood, nor of the will of the flesh, nor of the will of man, but of God" (John 1:12, 13). "Jesus answered, Verily, verily, I say unto thee, Except a man be born of water and of the Spirit, he cannot enter into the kingdom of God. That which is born of the flesh is flesh; and that which is born of the Spirit is spirit. Marvel not that I said unto thee, Ye must be born again. The wind bloweth where it listeth, and thou hearest the sound thereof, but canst not tell whence it cometh, and whither it goeth: so is every one that is born of the Spirit" (John 3:5-8). "I am come that they might have life, and that they might have it more abundantly" (John 10:10). "For in Christ Jesus neither circumcision availeth anything, nor uncircumcision, but a new creature" (Gal. 6:15). "Not by works of righteousness which we have done, but according to his mercy he saved us, by the washing of regeneration, and renewing of the Holy Ghost" (Titus 3:5). "Therefore if any man be in Christ, he is a new creature: old things are passed away; behold, all things are become new" (2 Cor. 5:17). "Whereby are given unto us exceeding great and precious promises: that by these ye might be partakers of the divine nature, having escaped the corruption that is in the world through lust" (2 Peter 1:4).

The reality of this mighty transformation is in no way evident in present visible things, but must be accepted by faith. It is no less than a translation from the kingdom of Satan into the kingdom of Christ, "who hath delivered us from the power of darkness, and hath translated us into the kingdom of his dear Son" (Col. 1:13). And by it one is said to be delivered from this present evil age: "Who gave himself for our sins, that he might deliver us from this present evil world [age]. According to the will of God and our Father" (Gal. 1:4), and, also, according to the above passage, "to have escaped the corruption that is in the world" (Satanic system).

The new life that is thus imparted is none other than the very life of Christ: "Now if any man have not the Spirit of Christ, he is none of his" (Rom. 8:9). "To whom God would make known what is the riches of the glory of this mystery among the Gentiles; which is Christ in you, the hope of glory" (Col. 1:27). "I live; yet not I, but Christ liveth in me" (Gal. 2:20). "Examine yourselves, whether ye be in the faith; prove your own selves. Know ye not your own selves, how that Jesus Christ is in you, except ye be reprobates?" (2 Cor. 13:5).

The third great fact of the believer's present position in separation from this world is that the Holy Spirit is given unto him, at the moment of his regeneration, to indwell him, in place of the energizing power of Satan who "worketh" with energy in the children of disobedience: "The love of God is shed abroad in our hearts by the Holy Ghost which is given unto us" (Rom. 5:5). "Now we have received, not the spirit of the world, but the Spirit which is of God; that we might know the things that are freely given to us of God" (1 Cor. 2:12). "What? know ye not that your body is the temple of the Holy Ghost which is in you, which ye have of God, and ye are not your own?" (1 Cor. 6:19).

Another phase of the believer's position is revealed in the fact that he is said to be a citizen of heaven, his home center or citizenship having been moved there from the earth. His name would, therefore, appear only among the celestial beings, in any true census of the universe. The reality of this unseen relationship is brought out in several passages: "For our citizenship is in heaven; from whence also we wait for a Savior, the Lord Jesus Christ: who shall fashion anew the body of our humiliation, that it may be conformed to the body of his glory, according to the working whereby he is able even to subject all things unto himself" (Phil. 3:20, R.V.). "For ye know that if our earthly house of this tabernacle were dissolved, we have a building of God, an house not made with hands, eternal in the heavens. For in this we groan, earnestly desiring to be clothed upon with our house which is from heaven: if so be that being clothed we shall not be found naked. For we that are in this tabernacle do groan, being burdened: not for that we would be unclothed, but clothed upon, that mortality might be swallowed up of life. Now he that hath wrought us for the selfsame thing is God, who also hath given unto us the earnest of the Spirit. Therefore we are always confident, knowing that, whilst we are at home in the body, we are absent from the Lord: (For we walk by faith, not by sight:) we are confident, I say, and willing rather to be absent from the body, and to be present with the Lord" (2 Cor. 5:1-8).

Again, as to the believer's position in that which is termed in Ephesians "the heavenly *places*"—though the supplying of the word "places" is misleading. The meaning of the word "heavenly" is not so much of locality as of experience, as is indicated by the use of the same word in other passages where the believer is said to be 'heavenly' in standing and relationship (Heb. 3:1; Eph. 2:6. See also Matt. 18:35; John 3:12; 1 Cor. 15:48).

Dr. C. I. Scofield makes the following statement on this important phase of the believer's position:

"The Christian is 'heavenly' by calling (Heb. 3:1), by citizenship (Phil. 3:20), by inheritance (1 Pet. 1:4) and by resurrection life (Eph. 2:6), as a member of that body of which the Head is actually in heaven. The heavenly (or 'in heavenly places,') therefore, is the sphere of the believer's present association with Christ. This is shown by the constant context, 'in Christ Jesus.' The believer is now associated with Christ in life (Col. 3:4; 1 John 5:11, 12), position (Eph. 2:6), suffering (Rom. 8:18; 2 Tim. 2:11, 12; Col. 1:24; Phil. 1:29) service (John 17:18; Matt. 28:18-20), and betrothal (2 Cor. 11:1-3).

"The believer is to be associated with Christ in glory (John 17:22; Rom. 8:18; Col. 3:4), inheritance (Rom. 8:17), authority (Matt. 19:28; Rev. 3:21), and marriage (Eph. 5:22, 33; Rev. 19:1-9).

"The believer's 'spiritual blessings' (Eph. 1:3), therefore, are to be possessed or experienced only as he lives in the sphere of his joint life, joint position, joint suffering, joint service and joint marriage pledge with Christ. In so far as he lives as a natural man whose interests are earthly, and avoids the path of co-service and (if need be) co-suffering, he will know nothing experimentally of the exalted blessing of Ephesians. 'It is sufficient that the servant be as his Master.' Christ took account of Himself as a heavenly Being come down to earth to do His Father's will."[2]

Thus it may be seen that the believer is not only a citizen of heaven, but that he has also been brought into a position where many privileges of the heavenly experience are open to him.

In like manner, the believer's position in relation to this world is not only a separation from the world by nature and purpose; but he is also said to be a stranger and a pilgrim among the

---

2. *Scofield Bible Correspondence Course*, Book 2; page 288.

inhabitants of this dark age. "But ye are a chosen generation, a royal priesthood, an holy nation, a peculiar people; that ye should shew forth the praises of him who hath called you out of darkness into his marvellous light: which in time past were not a people, but are now the people of God: which had not obtained mercy, but now have obtained mercy. Dearly beloved, I beseech you as strangers and pilgrims, abstain from fleshly lusts, which war against the soul; having your conversation honest among the Gentiles" (1 Peter 2:9-12). The same expression of "strangers and pilgrims" is used, also, in regard to the faith descendants of Abraham: "These all died in faith, not having received the promises, but having seen them afar off, and were persuaded of them, and embraced them, and confessed that they were strangers and pilgrims on the earth" (Heb. 11:13). This same wide difference between the people of this world and the people of God is also stated in passages where the world is understood to be the system over which Satan now rules: He that loveth his life shall lose it; and he that hateth his life in this world [*Satanic system*] shall keep it unto life eternal" (John 12:25). "Ye adulterers and adulteresses, know ye not that the friendship of the world is enmity with God? Whosoever therefore will be a friend of the world [*Satanic system*] is the enemy of God" (James 4:4). "Love not the world [*Satanic system*], neither the things that are in the world. If any man love the world, the love of the Father is not in him. For all that is in the world, the lust of the flesh, and the lust of the eyes, and the pride of life, is not of the Father, but is of the world. And the world passeth away, and the lust thereof: but he that doeth the will of God abideth forever" (1 John 2:15-17).

The word "lust" constantly used in description of the Satanic system has a much larger meaning in the scriptures than its present popular use, where it refers only to that which is sensual. In these quoted passages it refers to the whole Satan-inspired ambition of humanity, and includes their principle of self-help, and their struggle for all that is highest and best to them. The lust of the world is unlawful, because it disregards the truth of God; and it is related to that which is physical, because it magnifies the finite being and its resources.

Two other striking passages concerning the relation of the

believer to the world are here given: "Herein is our love made perfect, that we may have boldness in the day of judgment: because as he is, so are we in this world [*Satanic system*] (1 John 4:17). "As thou hast sent me into the world [*Satanic system*], even so have I also sent them into the world [*Satanic system*]" (John 17:18).

The last revelation concerning the believer's position to be mentioned here, is in regard to his service for the world. The unbounded love of God has called him into fellowship with Christ in the great work of this age; and in that connection he is under commission to evangelize, by a process of witnessing, to the uttermost parts of the world. The language of the inspired Book describes such witnesses as "Ambassadors for Christ:" "Now then we are ambassadors for Christ, as though God did beseech you by us: we pray you in Christ's stead, be ye reconciled to God" (2 Cor. 5:20). And the ambassador's message is also given in the next verse of the same passage: "For he hath made him to be sin for us, who knew no sin; that we might be made the righteousness of God in him" (we who knew no righteousness).

Nowhere does the saint need more definite teaching of the Spirit than in regard to the relation he sustains to this world. In spite of the similarity of his earth-life to that of the world's people, he must reckon himself to be dead in Christ and raised to newness of life. Expecting the world to misunderstand him and even to hate him, he must wisely walk before them who are "without." He is called upon to "use this world but not to abuse it;" and that which is of itself pure and good may become undesirable to him at times, because its use would further the interests of Satan.

Some have taken the extreme position of assigning to Satan the material universe and everything that is in the world today, not recognizing the fact that no material or physical thing is evil of itself. God created all things good. Satan has created nothing, and his present relation to the world is only as a permitted usurper who appropriates and devastates the things of God in the interests of his own ambition. He is the file-leader in a great rebellion against the government of God; but the natural universe belongs primarily to God, the Creator; and by title of inheritance, it belongs also to the child of God, as it is written, "Therefore let no man glory in men. For all things are yours; whether Paul, or Apollos, or Cephas, or the world, or life, or death, or things present, or things to come; all are yours; and ye are Christ's; and Christ is God's" (1 Cor. 3:21-23). Yet, since Satan is making use of many good things to cover his evil purpose, the child of God must, for the present, discern the hidden evil and in loyalty to his Lord reject everything that may further the workings of Satan. The Bible is very clear on this point, and discusses one issue as an example of all similar issues. This discussion in scripture is about food which of itself is perfectly good, but may be a means of great harm when associated with the purposes of evil. The passages are as follows:

"Let us not therefore judge one another any more: but judge this rather, that no man put a stumbling block or an occasion to fall in his brother's way. I know, and am persuaded by the Lord Jesus, that there is nothing unclean of itself: but to him that esteemeth anything to be unclean, to him it is unclean. But if thy brother be grieved with thy meat, now walkest thou not charitably. Destroy not him with thy meat, for whom Christ died. Let not then your good be evil spoken of: for the kingdom of God is not meat and drink; but righteousness, and peace, and joy in the Holy Ghost. For he that in these things serveth Christ is acceptable to God, and approved of men. Let us therefore follow after the things which make for peace, and things wherewith one may edify another. For meat destroy not the work of God. All things indeed are pure; but it is evil for that man who eateth with offence. It is good neither to eat flesh nor to drink wine, nor anything whereby thy brother stumbleth, or is offended, or is made weak" (Rom. 13-21). "What say I then that the idol is anything, or that which is offered in sacrifice to idols is anything? But I say, that the things which the Gentiles sacrifice, they sacrifice to devils and not to God: and I would not that ye should have fellowship with devils. Ye cannot drink the cup of the Lord, and the cup of devils: ye cannot be partakers of the Lord's table, and of the table of devils. Do we provoke the Lord to jealousy? Are we stronger than he? All things are lawful for me, but all things are not expedient: all things are lawful for me, but all things edify not. Let no man seek his own, but every man another's wealth. Whatsoever is sold in the shambles, that eat, asking no question for conscience sake: for the earth is the Lord's, and the fullness thereof. If any of them that believe not bid you to a feast, and ye be disposed to go; whatsoever is set before you, eat, asking no question for conscience sake. But if any man say unto you, This is offered in sacrifice unto idols, eat not for his sake that shewed it, and for conscience sake: for the earth is the Lord's and the fullness thereof: conscience, I say, not thine own, but of the other: for why is my liberty judged of another man's conscience? For if I by grace be a partaker, why am I evil spoken of for that for which I give thanks? Whether therefore ye eat, or drink, or whatsoever ye do, do all to the glory of God. Give none offence, neither to the Jews, nor to the Gentiles, nor to the church of God: even as I please all men in all things, not seeking mine own profit, but the profit of many, that they may be saved" (1 Cor. 10:19-33).

The question becomes a practical one, in view of the present progress in discovery, science, and psychology. A theory must not be rejected because it is new or mysterious; for the marvellous inventions of the age are often as useful in spreading the Gospel as in furthering the interests of Satan. The newly acquired knowledge of the universe may be as valuable to the progress of good as to the advancement of evil.

There can be but one final test as to what shall be accepted and what shall be rejected, and that must be made by the individual alone before God (Rom. 14:22). In connection with any such question we may ask, "Is the real work of redemption hindered, or its true basis rejected? Is this a direct denial of the truth, by which souls will be hindered, or is it a counterfeit which may decoy them away from their only hope in the priceless blood of the cross? Beyond this, a child of God may safely be "all things to all men that he may save some."

The Christian can see more of beauty in the world, make larger use of its learning, and more fully appreciate its good, than can the children of this age: yet he must now, above all things else, be content with his limited commission, and be jealous for the interests of his Lord. Much of his present perplexity would be relieved if he could but realize that he is temporarily tenting where an enemy rules, and where he is the object of that enemy's fiery darts, yet hedged about by the omnipotence of God; called to bear the one message of redemption by the cross, in the capacity and hidden dignity of an ambassador from the throne of the Most High; even now possessing a glory which shall soon be unveiled in the presence of his Lord; and waiting for that morning when his Lord shall come again and receive him unto Himself.

The Christian's position, then, is one of absolute security because of his vital union with Christ, the infinite power of the Spirit, and the unfailing grace of God. Yet it is permitted that the child of God shall be the target of the "fiery darts of the wicked one." It is revealed that, to some extent, his present strength and future reward are the result of this unceasing warfare. The conflict is real; but beyond it all there is the revelation that these eternal positions can never be moved. If they depended in the slightest degree upon the merit of any man they could never be attained, and much less maintained. They remain because they are founded on the unchanging and unchangeable Person of the Lord Jesus Christ.

12

The Believer's Present Victory

An exalted position is usually accompanied by great responsibility. This is certainly true, according to the Scriptures, in the case of the believer in his heavenly position. For when he is seen as a citizen of heaven, and a partaker of those associations, he is also required both by scripture and by reason to "walk worthy of the calling wherewith he is called." The statement of these heavenly demands upon the child of God forms a distinct body of truth, and there are at least three such bodies of truth in the Bible, each appearing as a rule of conduct for some special people in some particular time. The Mosaic Law was given primarily to God's ancient people through Moses; but it has a message still, as it reflects the holiness of God and prepares for the salvation which is in Christ. In like manner the "Sermon on the Mount" with the injunctions of John the Baptist and the early teachings of Christ were given with the coming kingdom age in view and, therefore, form an important revelation in regard to that time when "all shall know the Lord from the least unto the greatest." Though there are some common principles running through all these separate teachings, those scriptures which apply directly to the people of this parenthetical age of the Church will be found only in portions of the Gospels, and in the Epistles of the New Testament.

No appreciation of the provisions of God for a victorious life can be had until the demands which the believer's position imposes are realized. These demands are in no way the standards of the world, for the believer is not only a citizen of heaven in position, but is called upon even now to fulfil all the standards of that sphere. As an illustration of this fact, a few of these heavenly ideals and injunctions are given here: "I beseech you therefore, brethren, by the mercies of God, that ye present your bodies a living sacrifice, holy, acceptable unto God, which is your reasonable service" (Rom. 12:1). "Rejoice evermore. Pray without ceasing. In everything give thanks: for this is the will of God in Christ Jesus concerning you." . . . "Abstain from all appearance of evil" (1 Thess. 5:16-18, 22). "But the fruit of the Spirit is love, joy, peace, longsuffering, gentleness, goodness, faith, meekness, temperance: against such there is no law" (Gal. 5:22, 23). "I therefore, the prisoner of the Lord, beseech you that ye walk worthy of the vocation wherewith ye are called, with all lowliness and meekness, with longsuffering, forbearing one another in love; endeavouring to keep the unity of the Spirit in the bond of peace" (Eph. 4:1-3). "And grieve not the Holy Spirit of God, whereby ye are sealed unto the day of redemption" (Eph. 4:30). "Wherefore be ye not unwise, but understanding what the will of the Lord is. And be not drunk with wine, wherein is excess; but be filled with the Spirit; speaking to yourselves in psalms and hymns and spiritual songs, singing and making melody in your heart to the Lord; giving thanks always for all things unto God and the Father in the name of our Lord Jesus Christ" (Eph. 5:17-20). "Wherefore take unto you the whole armour of God, that ye may be able to withstand in the evil day, and having done all, to stand" (Eph. 6:13). "If ye then be risen with Christ, seek those things which are above, where Christ sitteth on the right hand of God. Set your affection on things above, not on things on the earth" (Col. 3:1, 2).

These requirements are evidently heavenly in character, and demand nothing less than that which is becoming to that sphere. They are, therefore, beyond human strength; for what human power is able to "give thanks always for all things"? Or to avoid grieving the Holy Spirit? Who can be filled with the Spirit, or rejoice in tribulation? In fact, these demands are often treated as impractical ideals, rather than present requirements, while in reality they are binding on every child of God. To fail in them at any point, will not unsave one (Rom. 4:5) but that failure will profane the heavenly citizenship, dishonor God in whose grace he is standing (Rom. 5:2), and give the enemy occasion to accuse the brethren before God; for Satan judges the Christian according to the basis of the heavenly ideals rather than according to the standards of earth. No one can contemplate these impossible responsibilities without a sense of utter helplessness and insufficiency.

Again, the believer must not only meet the impossible demands of a heavenly position, but he is called upon to face a world-ruling foe, who with all his kingdom and power is seeking to break and mar that life into which the divine nature has been received. The revelation that Satan is going about as a roaring lion, seeking whom he may devour, presents a truth that should disarm the believer of all self-confidence and cause him to dread, above all things else, the subtle devices of this foe. In this connection Ephesians 6:10-12, R.V., may well be restated: "Finally, brethren, be strong in the Lord, and in the strength of his might. Put on the whole armour of God, that ye may be able to stand against the wiles of the devil. For our wrestling is not against flesh and blood, but against the principalities, against the powers, against the world rulers of this darkness, against the spiritual host of wickedness in the heavenlies." In view of this opposition of Satan, it is still more evident that the requirements of the Christian life are beyond any human power.

So, also, there is a fallen human nature within the child of God which is prone to dishonor God, and is itself beyond the control of the human will. This important and much misunderstood truth is taken up at length in Romans 7:14-25: "For we know that the law is spiritual: but I am carnal, sold under sin. For that which I do I allow not: for what I would, that do I not; but what I hate, that do I. If then I do that which I would not, I consent unto the law that it is good. Now then it is no more I that do it, but sin that dwelleth in me. For I know that in me (that is, in my flesh), dwelleth no good thing: for to will is present with me; but how to perform that which is good I find not. For the good that I would I do not: but the evil which I would not, that I do. Now if I do that I would not, it is no more I that do it, but sin that dwelleth in me. I find then a law, that, when I would do good, evil is present with me. For I delight in the law of God after the inward man: but I see another law in my members, warring against the law of my mind, and bringing me into captivity to the law of sin which is in my members. O wretched man that I am! Who shall deliver me from the body of this death? I thank God through Jesus Christ our Lord. So then with the mind I myself serve the law of God; but with the flesh the law of sin."

This battle between the old nature and the new is, then, never gained for God by human power or by religious exercise: but through the power of the indwelling Spirit alone.

Thus the believer, as he contemplates his heavenly responsibility, is confronted with a threefold impossibility. First, the heavenly position demands a manner of life which is beyond any human possibility. Second, the enemy is stronger than he, and can thwart every resolution. Third, the believer's fallen nature entices him to do positive evil when he would do good. Notwithstanding this threefold impossibility, there is a clear call to a victorious life, wherein every thought is brought into captivity to the obedience of Jesus Christ (2 Cor. 10:5), and if the believer fails by one degree, he will dishonor the God who has called him.

Where, then, is the relief from this dilemma? It is found only in the power of the Spirit. God has provided a complete salvation from the dominion and power of evil, which is a real victory—the only victory for the believer in this present life and conflict. It is a second form or tense of salvation, for it is possible to be saved from the condemnation and penalty of sin, and still to be under its dominion and power. Salvation from the power of the world, the flesh, and the devil, may be secured as freely and completely as the salvation from the penalty of sin, and on the same terms; yet its terms and conditions are so unlike the methods of the world that often it seems unreal, even to Christians.

No instructed person expects to be free from condemnation, or justified before God, by virtue of his moral character; nor can there be freedom from the power of sin by virtue of the resolutions of the human will. Though the Christian life is impossible to human strength, it is within the power of God; and He offers to supply all that He requires, even to the measure of a completely victorious life. Since it is necessarily a divine undertaking, the human part can be no more than an attitude of expectation or faith toward God—an attitude which reckons self to be helpless, and God alone to be sufficient. It is a perpetual realization of the principle of faith and, therefore, at every point contradicts Satan's principle of self-help.

Here, as in every human effort to be God-like, Satan's ideals and methods are so thrust upon the world that the natural dependence of the creature upon the Creator is made to seem to be a weak and unreasonable thing. In spite of the teachings of scripture, this worldly mind has found a place in the church. It is often as difficult to inspire true expectation toward God in the Christian mind in the matter of daily victory, as it is to move the self-righteous and self-sufficient sinner to believe on Christ for regeneration.

True dependence upon the sufficiency of God is thus born through a vision of the utter inability of the natural man to meet the demands of the heavenly citizenship. The world-citizen may wrestle against flesh and blood to realize his moral ideals; but he has no heavenly standards to fulfill, no mighty foe to face, and no conflict of natures. Therefore, his low ideals may often be reached by virtue of his own resolution and will. Especially will this method be adequate for the unregenerate, because the energizing power of Satan is working in him to cause him both to will and to do the purpose of Satan (Eph. 2:2), but the faith principle is the only possible way to victory for the child of God, and it must be faith alone.

As the soul may be eternally lost, while calling upon God to help him save himself, so the saint who only seeks the assistance of God in the exercise of his own power toward a correct manner of life, may be constantly a dishonor to God. The principles of faith and of works can no more be mixed in the one case than in the other. They both present human impossibilities and, therefore, demand the power of God. The scriptures are clear on this point, both in precept and example:

First, *the power of God is the believer's sufficiency for meeting the heavenly demands:* "For it is God which worketh in you both to will and to do of his good pleasure" (Phil. 2:13). "Not that we are sufficient of ourselves to think anything as of ourselves: but our sufficiency is of God" (2 Cor. 3:5). "But by the grace of God, I am what I am: and his grace which was bestowed upon me was not in vain; but I laboured more abundantly than they all: yet not I, but the grace of God which was with me" (1 Cor. 15:10). "Are ye so foolish? Having begun in the Spirit, are ye now made perfect by the flesh?" (Gal. 3:3). "Finally my brethren, be strong in the Lord, and in the power of his might" (Eph. 6:10). The latter passage is but the natural culmination of the whole revelation of the believer's citizenship and its responsibilities. Therefore, the final counsel is to be strong in the Lord and in the power of His might.

Second, *the conflict with the enemy can be a victory only by the power of God.* A remarkable revelation is given in the Scriptures of the attitude of the angels toward Satan, and this attitude may well be considered by fallen man. In Jude 9, Michael, the archangel, is seen in controversy with Satan over the body of Moses. There is no revelation as to the time or the occasion of this controversy. It is stated that Moses was buried in secret and was later seen in his transfigured and glorified body, so that it is possible that the removal of the body of Moses from the domain of Satan was the occasion referred to here. The passage is as follows: "Yet Michael, the archangel, when contending with the devil he disputed about the body of Moses, durst not bring against him a railing accusation, but said, The Lord rebuke thee." In like manner in 2 Peter 2:10, the false teachers of the end of this age are said to disregard the heavenly powers (evidently evil) which angels dare not do. "But chiefly them that walk after the flesh in the lust of uncleanness, and despise government. Presumptuous are they, self willed, they are not afraid to speak evil of dignities. Whereas angels, which are greater in power and might, bring not railing accusation against them before the Lord." There is probably a just regard, on the part of the angelic beings, for the fact that Satan is the "anointed" of God (Ezek. 28:14), as David would not lift up his hand against Saul because he was the "Lord's anointed" (1 Sam. 24:6). Christ is said to be anointed (Ps. 2:2); so also is the believer (1 John 2:27). But it is also shown here that the wisdom and strength of even Michael, the archangel, and all other celestial beings, is never lifted in conflict with Satan. They rely only upon the same power that is promised the believer, and well may the believer be instructed by their example.

There are two passages where the child of God is directed to resist the devil. The context, however, in both passages warns him that it must be in utter dependence upon the power of God. He must be wholly submitted to God and it must be done through a steadfastness of faith. The passages are as follows: "Submit yourselves therefore to God. Resist the devil, and he will flee from you" (James 4:7). "Be sober, be vigilant; because your adversary the devil, as a roaring lion, walketh about, seeking whom he may devour: whom resist steadfast in the faith" (1 Peter 5:8, 9). And the faith principle is mentioned among the believer's armor in Eph. 6:16 as the "shield of faith" by which all the fiery darts of the enemy are to be quenched.

Third, *true character may be realized by the power of God, in spite of the tendency of the fallen nature*. This character, however, is that which is directly promised by the power of God: "But the fruit of the Spirit is love, joy, peace, longsuffering, gentleness, goodness, faith, meekness, temperance" (Gal. 5:22, 23). "For the fruit of the Spirit is in all goodness and righteousness and truth" (Eph. 5:9). "Ye are of God, little children, and have overcome them: because greater is he that is in you, than he that is in the world" (1 John 4:4). Thus the true God-honoring character is seen to be the result of the power of God, and it is only possible to the one who has "ceased from his own labors and has entered into rest." "This is the victory that overcometh the world, even our faith" (1 John 5:4). This victory demands a constant exercise of faith. Faith is never finished here, and any true progress in the Christian life is "from faith to faith," and it is also said of the one whom God has constituted just that he shall "live by faith." It should be remembered that the conflict is really between Christ and Satan. "Greater is he that is in you than he that is in the world." The Christian's victory is gained by faith in Him.

The same objection is often raised against the application of the faith principle as a means to the consummation of a victorious life, as is raised against the same principle for regeneration. In this objection it is inferred that when this method is adopted, there is no adequate incentive or motive left for the individual. Such objections arise from a misunderstanding of this truth.

It is useless to undertake the impossible in any case; and in the matter of salvation from the penalty of sin, the only work which it is possible for God to accept as the ground of redemption is that which is already undertaken and fully completed by Christ on the cross. By this finished work the believer is provided with a perfect standing before God, and is raised to the exalted position of an ambassador for Christ. That privilege of service does not affect the grounds of his salvation, but opens to him the glorious possibility of rewards (1 Cor. 3:9-15). In the question of salvation from the power of sin, the human will may be employed as an instrument through which the power of God may be manifested. The following passages reveal how directly He proposes to be the real power in the believer's life: "For it is God which worketh in you both to will and to do of his good pleasure" (Phil. 2:13). "For though we walk in the flesh, we do not war after the flesh: (For the weapons of our warfare are not carnal, but mighty through God to the pulling down of strongholds;) casting down imaginations, and every high thing that exalteth itself against the knowledge of God, and bringing into captivity every thought to the obedience of Christ" (2 Cor. 10:3-5). "I can do all things through Christ which strengtheneth me" (Phil. 4:13). "For apart from me ye can do nothing" (John 15:5).

It is assumed that the believer has recognized the perfectness of the will of God and has thrown his whole being open to His power and guidance. As a little child may avail himself of the wisdom and experience of his parents through obedience, so the believer has become willing to do whatever the infinite wisdom and love of God may choose for him. When thus committed to the will of God, and in true faith depending on Him, the mighty power of the Spirit will work in him and through him to the glory of God. "This I say then, Walk in the Spirit, and ye shall not fulfil the lust of the flesh" (Gal. 5:16). "For the law of the Spirit of life in Christ Jesus hath made me free from the law of sin and death" (Rom. 8:2). Salvation in any form is, therefore, "not of works, lest any man should boast."[1]

It remains to be seen, in view of the perilous position of the

---

1. The Bible teaching concerning the power of God in the life of the believer is fully presented in the author's book, *He That Is Spiritual*.

believer in the enemy's land, that God has not only provided every needed force for conquest and victory, but has given positive promises for the security of the one whom He has received on the ground of the shed blood of Christ, "Hast not thou made an hedge about him, and about his house, and about all that he hath on every side?" (Job 1:10). "My Father, which gave them me, is greater than all; and no man [nothing], is able to pluck them out of my Father's hand" (John 10:29). "There hath no temptation taken you but such as is common to man: but God is faithful, who will not suffer you to be tempted above that ye are able; but will with the temptation also make a way to escape, that ye may be able to bear it" (1 Cor. 10:13). "Who shall lay anything to the charge of God's elect? It is God that justifieth. Who is he that condemneth? It is Christ that died, yea, rather that is risen again, who is even at the right hand of God, who also maketh intercession for us. Who shall separate us from the love of Christ? shall tribulation, or distress, or persecution, or famine, or nakedness, or peril, or sword? As it is written, For thy sake we are killed all the day long; we are accounted as sheep for the slaughter. Nay, in all these things we are more than conquerors through him that loved us. For I am persuaded that neither death, nor life, nor angels, nor principalities, nor powers, nor things present, nor things to come, nor height, nor depth, nor any other creature, shall be able to separate us from the love of God, which is in Christ Jesus our Lord."

An Appeal

This book will have accomplished its mission if you, its reader, are by it made more conscious of what it means to be translated from the power of darkness into the kingdom of God's dear Son. Will you not be more sure of your saving faith in Christ than of any other fact in your life, since upon this faith your eternity depends?

On the other hand, if you know you are saved, the ministry of this book has been accomplished if by its message you know more of the devices of the enemy of God, and are able to enter more intelligently into the way of escape which grace has provided.

"Now unto him that is able to keep you from falling, and to present you faultless before the presence of his glory with exceeding joy, to the only wise God our Savior, be glory and majesty, dominion and power, both now and ever, Amen."

Scripture Index

137

Subject Index